SELECTIONS FROM

100 greAtest Sa

Piano • Vocal • Guitar

MW00669203

100 greATEST SoNgS of the 90's

ISBN 978-1-4234-3663-8

HAL•LEONARD®
CORPORATION

7777 W. BLUEMOUND RD. P.O. BOX 13819 MILWAUKEE, WI 53213

Visit Hal Leonard Online at
www.halleonard.com

1	SMELLS LIKE TEEN SPIRIT	Nirvana
2	ONE*	U2
3	I WANT IT THAT WAY	Backstreet Boys
4	I WILL ALWAYS LOVE YOU	Whitney Houston
5	VOGUE	Madonna
6	BABY GOT BACK	Sir Mix-A-Lot
7	…BABY ONE MORE TIME	Britney Spears
8	WATERFALLS	TLC
9	LOSING MY RELIGION	R.E.M.
10	NOTHING COMPARES 2 U	Sinéad O'Connor
11	JEREMY	Pearl Jam
12	YOU OUGHTA KNOW	Alanis Morissette
13	NUTHIN' BUT A G THANG	Dr. Dre (featuring Snoop Doggy Dogg)
14	VISION OF LOVE	Mariah Carey
15	UNDER THE BRIDGE	Red Hot Chili Peppers
16	U CAN'T TOUCH THIS	MC Hammer
17	SAY MY NAME	Destiny's Child
18	ENTER SANDMAN*	Metallica
19	SABOTAGE	Beastie Boys
20	MMM BOP*	Hanson
21	MY HEART WILL GO ON (LOVE THEME FROM 'TITANIC')	Celine Dion
22	LOSER	Beck
23	WHAT A MAN	Salt-N-Pepa with En Vogue
24	JUMP AROUND	House of Pain
25	BLACK HOLE SUN	Soundgarden
26	MY NAME IS	Eminem
27	MR. JONES	Counting Crows
28	LIVIN' LA VIDA LOCA	Ricky Martin
29	ICE ICE BABY	Vanilla Ice
30	TEARIN' UP MY HEART	*NSYNC
31	CREEP	Radiohead
32	NO DIGGITY	BLACKstreet
33	WANNABE	Spice Girls
34	SEMI-CHARMED LIFE	Third Eye Blind
35	WONDERWALL	Oasis
36	GONNA MAKE YOU SWEAT (EVERYBODY DANCE NOW)	C+C Music Factory
37	GOOD RIDDANCE (TIME OF YOUR LIFE)	Green Day
38	GENIE IN A BOTTLE	Christina Aguilera
39	IRIS	Goo Goo Dolls
40	I WANNA SEX YOU UP	Color Me Badd
41	TWO PRINCES	Spin Doctors
42	SHINE	Collective Soul
43	MY LOVIN'	En Vogue
44	KILLING ME SOFTLY WITH HIS SONG	Fugees
45	ONLY WANNA BE WITH YOU	Hootie & the Blowfish
46	YOU'RE STILL THE ONE	Shania Twain
47	GOOD VIBRATIONS	Marky Mark and The Funky Bunch
48	3 AM	matchbox twenty
49	WHO WILL SAVE YOUR SOUL	Jewel
50	MAN IN THE BOX	Alice in Chains

51	CALIFORNIA LOVE (REMIX)	Tupac (featuring Dr. Dre and Roger Troutman)
52	FLY	Sugar Ray
53	O.P.P.	Naughty by Nature
54	ONE OF US	Joan Osborne
55	CRIMINAL	Fiona Apple
56	MAMA SAID KNOCK YOU OUT	L.L. Cool J
57	CAN I GET A . . .	Jay-Z featuring Amil and Ja Rule
58	DAMN, I WISH I WAS YOUR LOVER	Sophie B. Hawkins
59	BUDDY HOLLY	Weezer
60	POISON*	Bell Biv DeVoe
61	ALL I WANNA DO	Sheryl Crow
62	I ALONE	Live
63	MO' MONEY MO' PROBLEMS	The Notorious B.I.G. featuring Mase & Puff Daddy
64	PEACHES	The Presidents of the United States of America
65	THE HUMPTY DANCE	Digital Underground
66	I'LL BE	Edwin McCain
67	GROOVE IS IN THE HEART	Deee-Lite
68	GETTIN' JIGGY WIT IT	Will Smith
69	FREAK ON A LEASH	Korn
70	VIRTUAL INSANITY	Jamiroquai
71	TENNESSEE	Arrested Development
72	ONE WEEK	Barenaked Ladies
73	SEX AND CANDY	Marcy Playground
74	BELIEVE	Cher
75	JUMP	Kris Kross
76	RUN AROUND	Blues Traveler
77	IT WAS A GOOD DAY	Ice Cube
78	ARE YOU GONNA GO MY WAY*	Lenny Kravitz
79	BITCH	Meredith Brooks
80	I'M TOO SEXY	Right Said Fred
81	I DON'T WANT TO WAIT	Paula Cole
82	MIND PLAYING TRICKS ON ME	Geto Boys
83	CANNONBALL*	The Breeders
84	INFORMER	Snow
85	INSANE IN THE BRAIN	Cypress Hill
86	LINGER	The Cranberries
87	ACHY BREAKY HEART (DON'T TELL MY HEART)	Billy Ray Cyrus
88	BARELY BREATHING	Duncan Sheik
89	NEVER SAID	Liz Phair
90	YOU GET WHAT YOU GIVE	New Radicals
91	BUILDING A MYSTERY	Sarah McLachlan
92	911 IS A JOKE	Public Enemy
93	STAY	Lisa Loeb & Nine Stories
94	THE WAY	Fastball
95	THIS IS HOW WE DO IT	Montell Jordan
96	(CAN'T LIVE WITHOUT YOUR) LOVE AND AFFECTION	Nelson
97	GETT OFF	Prince & The New Power Generation
98	UNBELIEVABLE	EMF
99	THE RAIN (SUPA DUPA FLY)	Missy "Misdemeanor" Elliott
100	RICO SUAVE	Gerardo

*Omitted from this publication because of licensing restrictions.

ACHY BREAKY HEART
(Don't Tell My Heart)

Words and Music by
DON VON TRESS

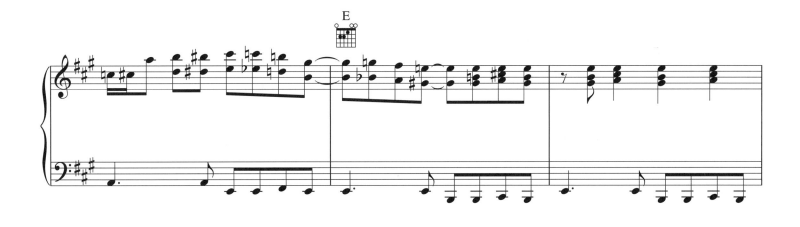

ALL I WANNA DO

Words and Music by KEVIN GILBERT,
DAVID BAERWALD, SHERYL CROW,
WYN COOPER and BILL BOTTRELL

(Spoken:) Hit it! This ain't no disco.   It ain't no country club either.

This is L.A.   1. "All I wan-na do __ is have __ a lit-tle

fun be-fore I die,"   says the man __ next to me   out of no - where, __

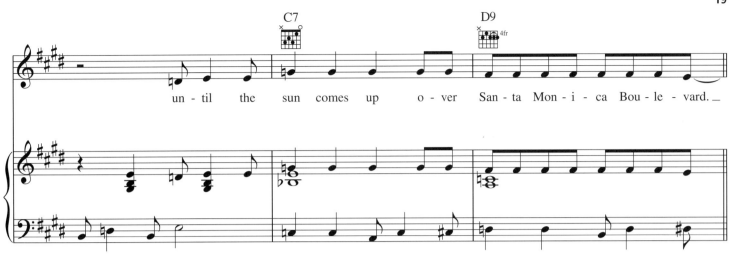

un - til   the   sun   comes   up   o - ver   San - ta   Mon - i - ca   Bou - le - vard. _

_ *(Vocal 1st time only)*

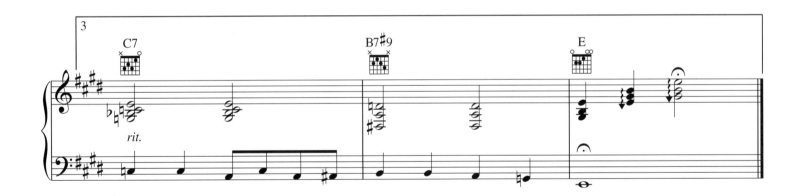

Additional Lyrics

3. I like a good beer buzz early in the morning,
   And Billy likes to peel the labels from his bottles of Bud
   And shred them on the bar.
   Then he lights every match in an oversized pack,
   Letting each one burn down to his thick fingers
   Before blowing and cursing them out.
   And he's watching the Buds as they spin on the floor.
   A happy couple enters the bar dancing dangerously close to one another.
   The bartender looks up from his want ads.
   Chorus

BABY GOT BACK

Words and Music by
ANTHONY L. RAY

Medium Rap tempo

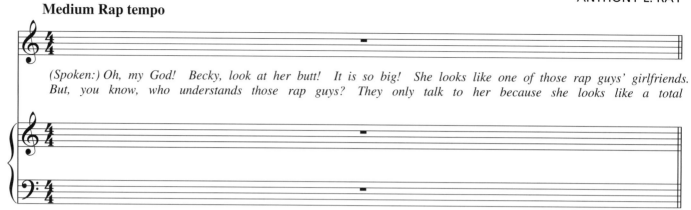

(Spoken:) Oh, my God! Becky, look at her butt! It is so big! She looks like one of those rap guys' girlfriends. But, you know, who understands those rap guys? They only talk to her because she looks like a total

prostitute, okay? I mean, her butt is just so
out there. I mean gross! Look!

big! I can't believe it's just so round! It's like
She's just so black! Rap: (See rap lyrics)

Figure A

Figure B

Ending

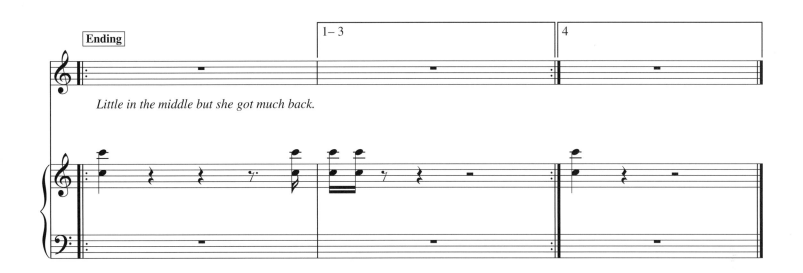

Little in the middle but she got much back.

Alternate Figures A and B throughout

Rap Lyrics

Rap 1: I like Big Butts and I cannot lie
you other Brothers can't deny
that when a girl walks in with an itty bitty waist
and a round thang in your face
You get sprung wanna pull up tough
'cause you noticed that butt was stuffed
deep in the jeans she's wearin'
And I'm hooked and I can't stop starin'
Oh, baby, I wanna get with ya
and take your picture
My home boys tried to warn me
But that butt you got makes "me so Horny"
OOOO rump of smooth skin
you say you wanna get in my Benz
well use me, use me
'cause you ain't that average groupie
I saw her dancin'
to hell with romancin'
She's sweatin' wet
got it going like a turbo Vette
I'm tired of Magazines
saying flat butts are the thing
take the average Black man and ask him that
she's gotta pack much back
Fellas (yeah) Fellas (yeah)
does your female got the butt (yeah)
tell 'em to shake it (shake it) shake it (shake it)
Shake that healthy butt
Baby's got back

Rap 2: I like 'em round and big
And when I'm throwin' a gig
I just can't help myself I'm acting like an animal
now here's my scandal
I wanna get you home and Uh
Double up Uh Uh
I ain't talkin' bout playboy
'cause silicone parts are made for toys
I want 'em real, thick and juicy
So fine that you'll see
Double Mix-A-Lot's in trouble
beggin' for a piece of that bubble
So I'm lookin' at rock videos
knock kneed bimbos walkin' like ho's
You can have them bimbos
I'll take my women like Flo Jo
A word to the thick soul sisters I wanna get with ya
I won't cuss or hit ya
but I gotta be straight
when I say I wanna... 'til the break
of Dawn baby got it going on
a lot of wimps won't like this song
'cause them punks like to hit it & quit it
but I'd rather stay and play
'cause I'm long and I'm strong
and I'm down to get that friction on
Now Ladies (yeah) Ladies (yeah)
Do you wanna roll in my Mercedes (yeah)
then turn around stick it out
Even white boys got to shout
Baby's got back

Rap 3: So your girlfriend rolls a Honda
Playin' workout tapes by Fonda
but Fonda ain't got a motor in the back of her Honda
my Anaconda
don't want none
unless you got buns hun
You can do side bends or sit ups
but please don't lose that butt
some brothers wanna play that hard role
and tell you the butt ain't gold
so they toss it and leave it
and I pull up quick to retrieve it
so cosmo says you're fat
but I ain't down with that
'cause your waist is small and your curves are kickin'
and I'm thinkin' 'bout stickin'
to the beanpole dames in the Magazines
you ain't it miss thing
Gimmie a sister I can't resist her
red beans and rice didn't miss her
Some knuckleheads try to diss
'cause all his girls were on my list
he had game but he chose to hit 'em
and I pull up quick to get with 'em
so ladies if the butt is round
and you want a triple X throw down
dial 1-900-Mix-A-Lot
and kick them nasty thoughts
Baby's got back

To Ending

BITCH

Words and Music by MEREDITH BROOKS
and SHELLY PEIKEN

...BABY ONE MORE TIME

Words and Music by
MAX MARTIN

BARELY BREATHING

Words and Music by
DUNCAN SHEIK

BELIEVE

Words and Music by BRIAN HIGGINS,
STUART McLENNEN, PAUL BARRY,
STEPHEN TORCH, MATT GRAY
and TIM POWELL

*Recorded a half step higher.
**Vocal written one octave higher than sung.

BLACK HOLE SUN

Words and Music by
CHRIS CORNELL

Won't you come? _____

Won't you come? _____

Won't you come? _____

BUDDY HOLLY

Words and Music by
RIVERS CUOMO

Moderate Rock

What's with these hom — ies dis-sin' my girl? __
Don't you ev-er __ fear, I'm al-ways __ near.

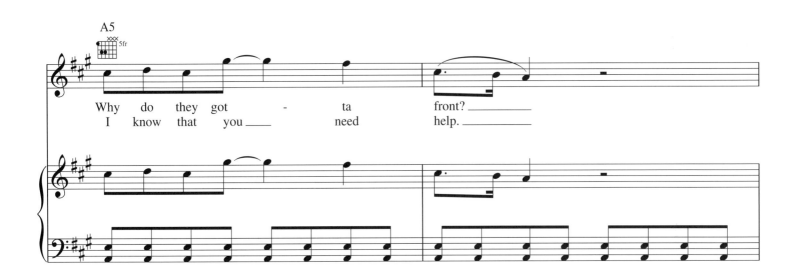

Why do they got - ta front? __
I know that you __ need help. __

What did we ev - er do to these guys __
Your tongue is twist - ed, your eyes are slit. __

BUILDING A MYSTERY

Words and Music by SARAH McLACHLAN
and PIERRE MARCHAND

CREEP

Words and Music by ALBERT HAMMOND,
MIKE HAZLEWOOD, Thomas Yorke,
RICHARD GREENWOOD, PHILIP SELWAY,
COLIN GREENWOOD and EDWARD O'BRIAN

CALIFORNIA LOVE
(Remix)

Words and Music by LARRY TROUTMAN,
ROGER TROUTMAN, WOODY CUNNINGHAM,
NORMAN DURHAM, RONNIE HUDSON
and MIKEL HOOKS

Rap Lyrics

Rap 1:
Now let me welcome everybody to the wild, wild west,
A state that's untouchable, like Eliot Ness.
The track hits your ear drum like a slug to the chest.
Pack a vest for your Jimmy in the city of sex.
We in that Sunshine State with a bomb ass hemp beat.
The state where ya never find a dance floor empty.
And pimps be on a mission for them greens.
Lean, mean money-makin' machines, servin' fiends.
I been in the game for ten years makin' rap tunes,
Ever since honeys was wearin' Sassoon.
Now it's ninety-five and they clock me and watch me.
Diamonds shinin', lookin' like I robbed Liberace.
It's all good, from Diego to tha Bay.
Your city is tha bomb, if your city makin' pay.
Throw up a finger if ya feel the same way.
Dre puttin' it down for Californ-i-a.
Chorus

Rap 2:
Out on bail, fresh outta jail, California dreamin',
Soon as I stepped on the scene, I'm hearin' hoochies screamin'.
Fiendin' for money and alcohol,
The life of a West Side playa where cowards die, and it's all a ball.
Only in Cali, where we riot, not rally to live and die in L.A.
We wearin' Chucks, not Ballies (that's right).
Dressed in Locs and Khaki suits and ride is what we do.
Flossin' but have caution, we collide with other crews.
Famous 'cause we program world-wide.
Let 'em recognize from Long Beach to Rosecrans.
Bumpin' and grindin' like a slow jam, it's West Side.
So you know the row won't bow down to no man.
Say what you say, but give me that bomb beat from Dre.
Let me serenade the streets of L.A.
From Oakland to Sacktown, the Bay Area and back down.
Cali is where they put they Mack down.
Give me love.
Chorus

Ending Rap Section:
Uh, yeah, uh, Long Beach in tha house, uh, yeah.
Oaktown, Oakland definitely in tha house, ha-ha-ha-ha.
Frisco, Frisco.
Hey, you know L.A. is up in this.
Pasadena, where you at?
Yeah, Inglewood, Inglewood always up to no good.
Even Hollywood tryin' to get a piece, baby.
Sacramento, Sacramento, where ya at? Yeah.
Throw it up, y'all, throw it up, throw it up.
I can't see ya.
California love.

CAN I GET A...

Words and Music by SHAWN CARTER,
IRVING LORENZO, JEFFREY ATKINS
and ROB MAYS

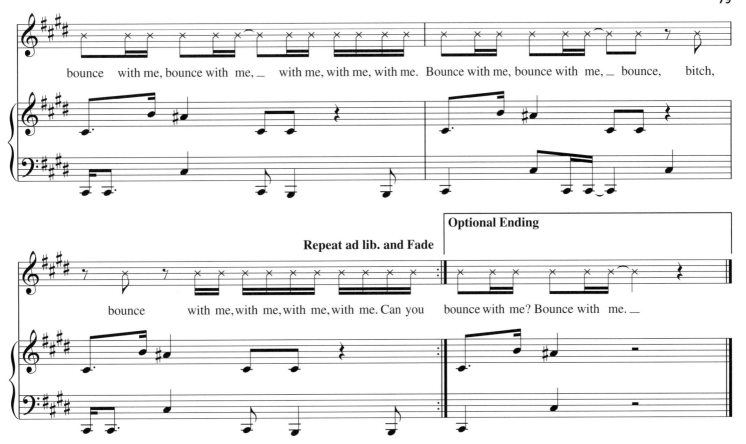

bounce with me, bounce with me, __ with me, with me, with me. Bounce with me, bounce with me, __ bounce, bitch,

Repeat ad lib. and Fade

Optional Ending

bounce with me, with me, with me, with me. Can you bounce with me? Bounce with me. __

Rap Lyrics

Rap 1: Can I hit in the morning
Without giving you half of my dough
And even worse if I was broke would you want me?
If I couldn't get you finer things
like all of them diamond rings bitches kill for,
would you still roll?
If we couldn't see the sun rising off the shore of Thailand,
Would you ride then, if I wasn't dropping?
If I wasn't a eight figure nigga by the name of Jigga,
would you come around me or would you clown me?
If I couldn't flow futuristic, would you
Put your two lips on my wood and kiss it - could you
See yourself with a nigga working harder than 9 to 5
Contend with six, two jobs to survive, or
Do you need a balla? So you can shop and tear the mall up?
Brag, tell your friends what I bought you
If you couldn't see yourself with a nigga when his dough is low
Baby girl, if this is so, yo...

Rap 2: You ain't gotta be rich but fuck that
How we gonna get around your bus pass
'Fore I put this pussy on your mustache
Can you afford me, my niggas breadwinners, never corny
Ambition makes me, so horny
Not the fussing and the fronting
If you got nothing, baby boy, you better
"Get up, get out and get something," shit!
I like a lot of Prada, Alize and Vodka
Late nights, candelight, then I tear the cock up
Get it up I put it down everytime it pop up, huh
I got to snap em, let it loose, then I knock ya
Feel the juice, then I got ya, when you produce a rocka
I let you meet momma and introduce you to poppa
My, coochie remains in a Gucci name
Never test my patience nigga, I'm high maintenance
High class, if you ain't rolling, bypass
If you ain't holdin, I dash yo...

Rap 3: It ain't even a question
How my dough flows, I'm good to these bad hoes
Like my bush wet and undry like damp clothes
What y'all niggas don't know, it's eazy to pimp a hoe
Bitches better have my money for sure
Before they go, running their mouth, promoting half
I be dicking they, back out, go ahead, let it out
I fucks with my gat out, bounce and leave a hundred
Makin them feel, slutted even if they don't want it
It's been so long
since I met a chick ain't on my tips but then I'm
Dead wrong, when I tell them be gone
So hold on to the feeling of flossing and platinum
'Cause from now on, you can witness Ja the icon
With hoodies and timbs on, 'cause I thugs my bitches
VeVe, studs my bitches, then we rob bitch niggas
I'm talkin about straight figures if you here, you with us
If not Boo, you know what, I still fucked you.

CRIMINAL

Words and Music by
FIONA APPLE

I've been a bad, __ bad __ girl; __   I've been care-less with a

DAMN, I WISH I WAS YOUR LOVER

Words and Music by
SOPHIE B. HAWKINS

D
A/C♯
Damn, I wish I was your lov - er.
Damn, I wish I was your lov - er. I'm
Bm
I'm on a sub - way and I'm com - in' up town.
get - tin' on my cam - el and I'm rid - in' up town, ooh.
D
A/C♯
Damn, I wish I was your lov - er.
Bm
Stand - ing on a street cor - ner, wait - ing for my life to change.

FLY

Words and Music by WILLIAM MARAGH,
ALAN SHACKLOCK, MARK McGRATH, RODNEY SHEPPARD,
JOSEPH NICHOL, STAN FRAZIER and MURPHY KARGES

Spread your love and fly, _____ spread your love and fly. _____

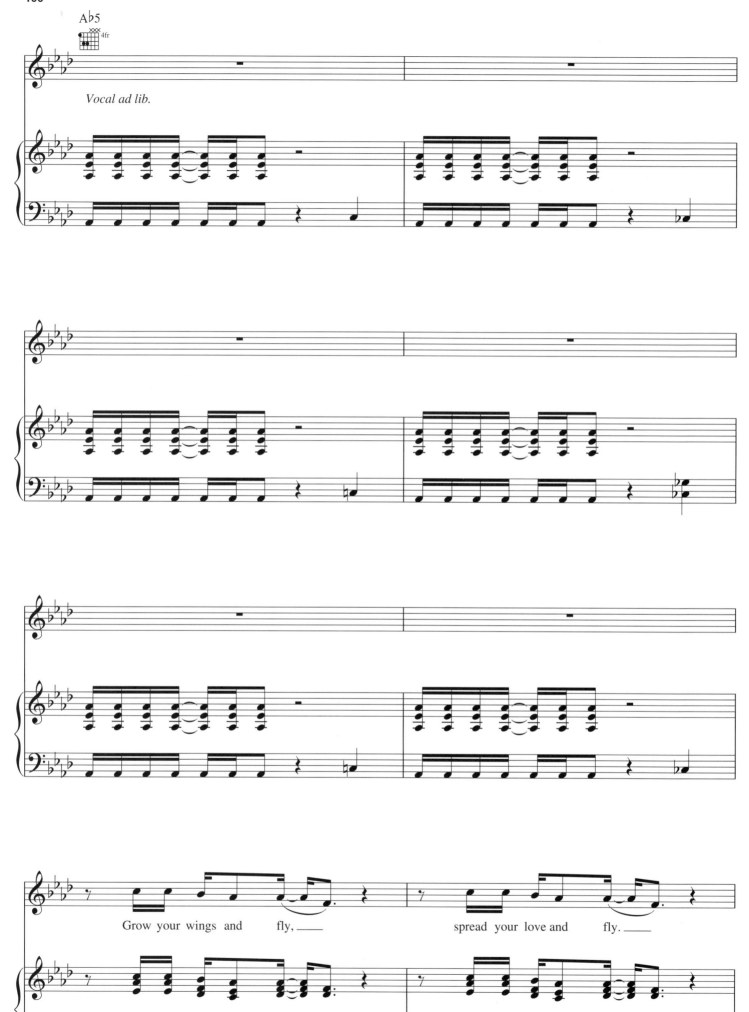

Grow your wings and fly, _____ spread your love and fly. _____

Let's take a tee-time on the bor-der-line.

FREAK ON A LEASH

Music and Lyrics by KORN

GENIE IN A BOTTLE

Words and Music by STEVE KIPNER,
DAVID FRANK and PAM SHEYNE

GOOD VIBRATIONS

Words and Music by DAN HARTMAN,
DONNIE WAHLBERG, MARK WAHLBERG
and AMIR SHAKIR

(Spoken:) Yeah. Can you feel it, baby? I can, too.

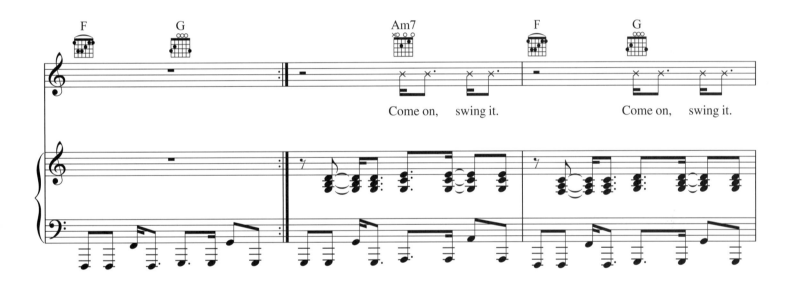

Come on, swing it. Come on, swing it.

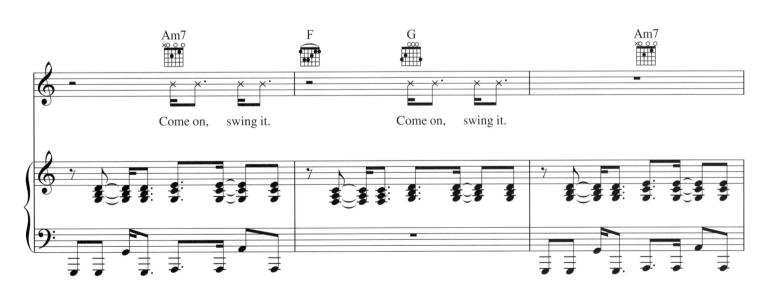

Come on, swing it. Come on, swing it.

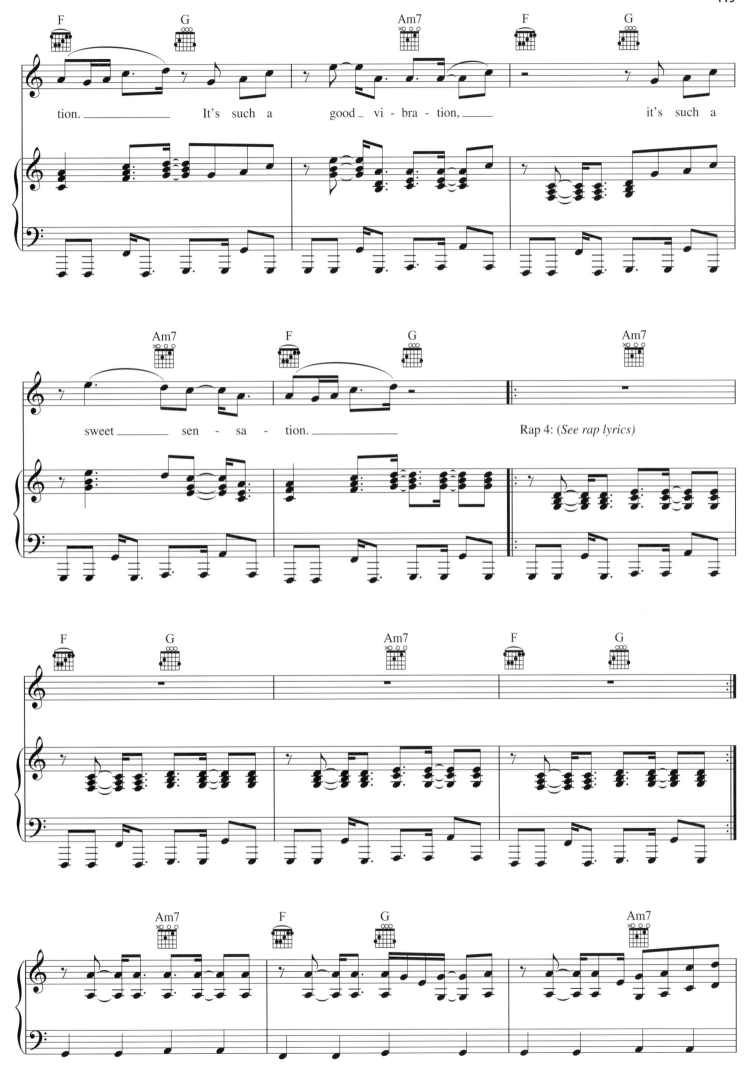

Rap Lyrics

Rap 1: Yo! It's about that time
To bring forth the rhythm and the rhyme
I'm a get mine so get yours
I wanna see sweat coming out your pores
On the house tip is how I'm swinging this
Strictly Hip-Hop boy, I ain't singing this
Bringing this to the entire nation
Black, white, red, brown
Feel the vibration

Rap 2: Vibrations good like Sunkist
Many wanna know who done this
Marky Mark and I'm here to move you
Rhymes will groove you
And I'm here to prove to you
That we can party on the positive side
And pump positive vibes
So come along for the ride
Making you feel the rhythm is my occupation
So feel the vibration

Rap 3: Donnie D's on the back up
Drug free, so put the crack up
No need for speed
I'm the anti D-R-U-G-G-I-E my
Body is healthy
My rhymes make me wealthy
And the Funky Bunch helps me
To bring you a show with no intoxication
Come on feel the vibration

Rap 4: Now the time has come for you to get up
The rest had you fed up but yo, I won't let up
On the rhythm and rhyme that's designed to
Make your behind move to what I'm inclined to
Pure Hip Hop, no sell out
If you ain't in it to win it
Then get the hell out
I command you to dance
I wanna see motivation
Come on now feel the vibration

GETT OFF

Words and Music by PRINCE
and ARLESTER CHRISTIAN

Moderately, with a heavy beat

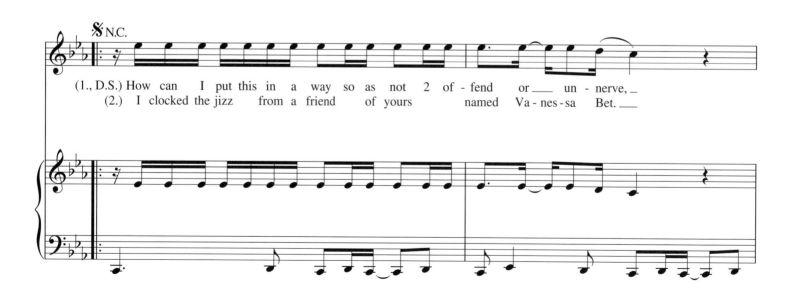

(1., D.S.) How can I put this in a way so as not 2 of - fend or ___ un - nerve, ___
(2.) I clocked the jizz from a friend of yours named Va - nes - sa Bet. ___

124

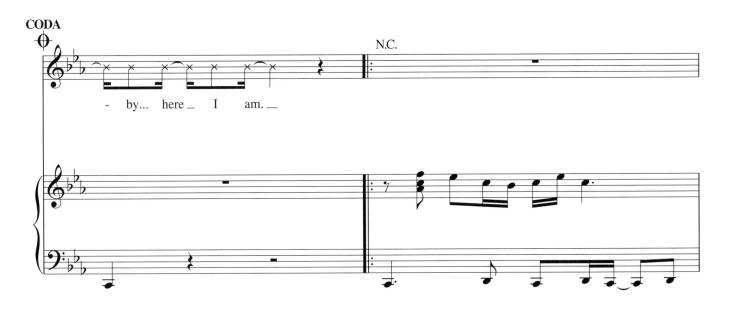

Rap Lyrics

Oooh I think I like it with the dress half on
I'll zip it far enough 2 see the crack-o'-dawn
Don't worry 'bout the bust, I'm gonna lock up every door
Then we can do it in the kitchen on the floor
Or in the bathroom standing on the tub and holding on the rod
In the closet underneath the clothes and oh, my God
In the bedroom on the dresser with your feet in the drawers
In the pantry on the shelf I guarantee U won't be bored
The pool table yeah, move the stix and put the 8-ball
Where it's sure 2 stick
Dudley do no wrong 2night if Nell just let him kick it

GETTIN' JIGGY WIT IT

Words and Music by NILE RODGERS,
BERNARD EDWARDS, WILL SMITH,
SAMUEL J. BARNES and J. ROBINSON

Rap Lyrics

Intro
(Loop)

Bring it.
Whoo!
Unh, unh, unh, unh
Hoo cah cah.
Hah hah, hah hah.
Bicka bicka bow bow bow,
Bicka bow bow bump bump.
What, what, what, what?
Hah hah hah hah.

Rap 1:
(Loop)

On your mark, ready, set, let's go.
Dance floor pro, I know you know
I go psycho when my new joint hit.
Just can't sit,
Gotta get jiggy wit it,
Ooh, that's it.
Now, honey, honey, come ride,
DKNY all up in my eye.
You gotta Prada bag with alotta stuff in it,
Give it to your friend, let's spin.
everybody lookin' at me,
Glancin' the kid,
Wishin' they was dancin' a jig
Here with this handsome kid.
Ciga-cigar right from Cuba-Cuba,
I just bite it.
It's for the look, I don't light it.
Illway the an-may on the ance-day oor-flay,
Givin' up jiggy, make it feel like foreplay.
Yo, my car-dee-o is Infinit-
Ha, ha.
Big Willie Style's all in it,
Gettin' jiggy wit it.

Refrain: Na na na na na na na, nana
(Loop) Na na na na nana.
Gettin' jiggy wit it.
(Repeat 3x)

Rap 2: What? You wanna ball with the kid?
(Loop) Watch your step, you might fall
Trying to do what I did.
Mama-unh, mama-unh, mama come closer
In the middle of the club with the rub-a-dub, uhn.
No love for the haters, the haters,
Mad cause I got floor seats at the Lakers.
See me on the fifty yard line with the Raiders.
Met Ali, he told me I'm the greatest.
I got the fever for the flavor of a crowd pleaser.
DJ, play another
From the prince of this.
Your highness,
Only mad chicks ride in my whips.
South to the west to the east to the north,
Bought my hits and watch 'em go off, a-go off.
Ah yes, yes y'all, ya don't stop.
Un the winter or the (summertime),
I makes it hot
Gettin' jiggy wit 'em.

Refrain

Rap 3: Eight-fifty I.S.; if you need a lift,
(Loop) Who's the kid in the drop?
Who else, Will Smith,
Livin' that life some consider a myth.
Rock from South Street to One Two Fifth.
Women used to tease me,
Give it to me now nice and easy
Since I moved up like George and Wheezy.
Cream to the maximum, I be askin' em,
"Would you like to bounce with the brother that's platinum?"
Never see Will attackin' 'em,
Rather play ball with Shaq and um,
Flatten 'em,
Psyche.
Kiddin',
You thought I took a spill
But I didn't.
Trust the lady of my life, she hittin'.
Hit her with a drop top with the ribbon,
Crib for my mom on the outskirts of Philly.
You, trying to flex on me?
Don't be silly,
Gettin' jiggy with it.

Refrain

GONNA MAKE YOU SWEAT
(Everybody Dance Now)

Words and Music by ROBERT CLIVILLES
and FREDERICK B. WILLIAMS

GROOVE IS IN THE HEART

Words and Music by KIER KIRBY,
DMITRY BRILL, TOWA TEI
and HERBIE HANCOCK

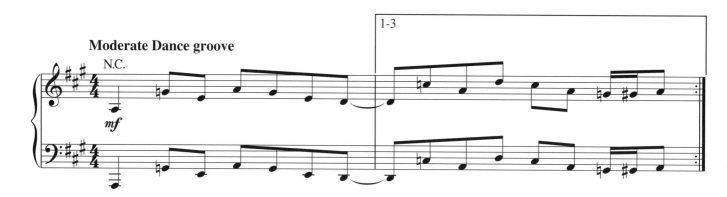

The chills that you spill __ up my back
groove I do deep-ly dig, __ no
Soul was on a roll. __

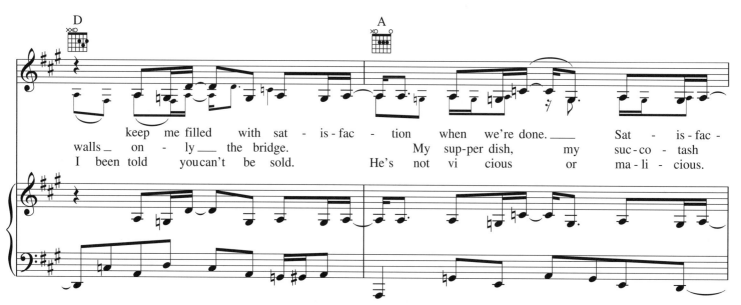

keep me filled with sat-is-fac-tion when we're done. __ Sat-is-fac-
walls __ on-ly __ the bridge. My sup-per dish, my suc-co-tash
I been told you can't be sold. He's not vi-cious or ma-li-cious.

Groove is in ___ the heart. _____

Groove is in ___ the heart. _____

Groove is in ___ the heart. _____

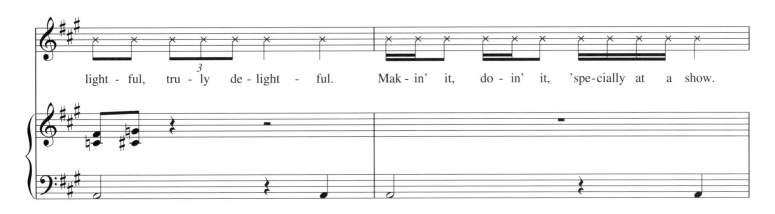

light - ful, tru - ly de - light - ful. Mak - in' it, do - in' it, 'spe-cially at a show.

Feel - in' kind - a high like a Hen - drix phase. Mu - sic makes most - ly move like a maze.

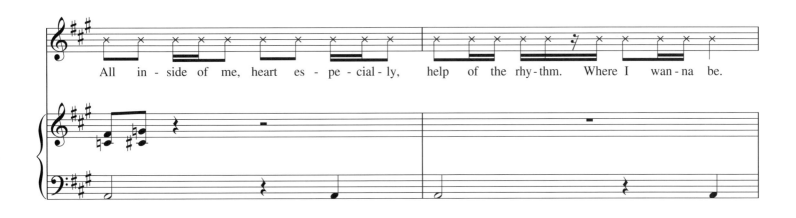

All in - side of me, heart es - pe - cial - ly, help of the rhy - thm. Where I wan - na be.

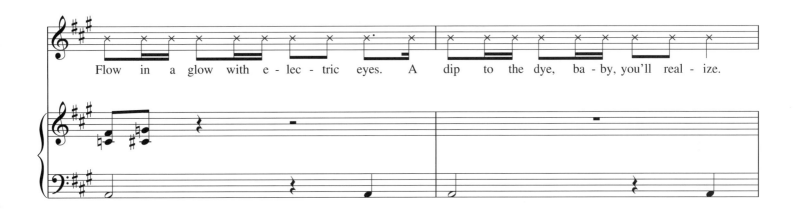

Flow in a glow with e - lec - tric eyes. A dip to the dye, ba - by, you'll real - ize.

Wait 'til you see the funk-y side of me. Ba - by, you'll see that rhy-thm is a key.

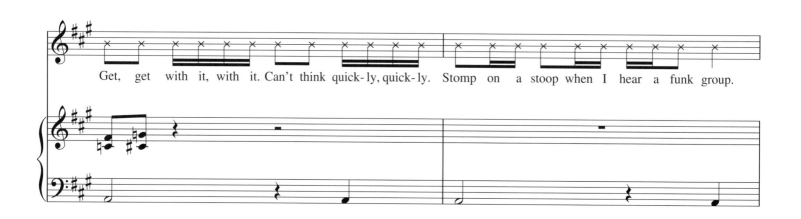

Get, get with it, with it. Can't think quick-ly, quick-ly. Stomp on a stoop when I hear a funk group.

Play-in' pied pip - er. Fol-low what's true. Ba - by, just sing a - bout the groove.

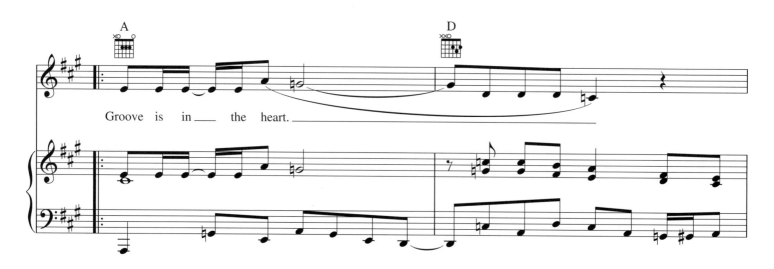

Groove is in ___ the heart. ___

THE HUMPTY DANCE

Words and Music by WILLIAM COLLINS,
GREGORY JACOBS, GEORGE CLINTON
and WALTER MORRISON

Oh, oh, do me, ba - by. Oh, oh, do me, ba-

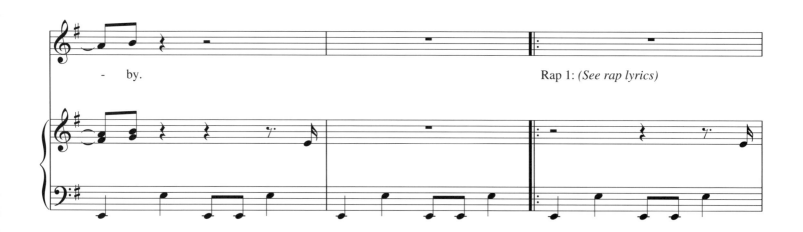

- by.

Rap 1: *(See rap lyrics)*

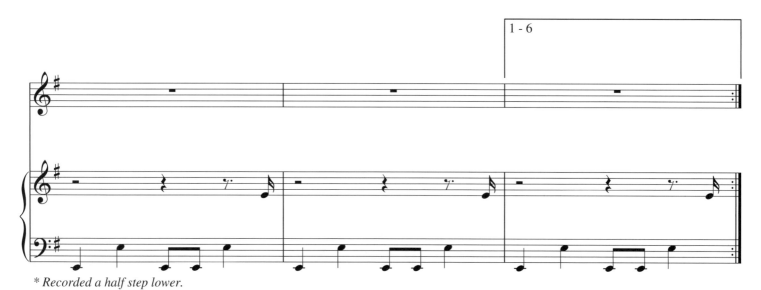

1 - 6

* Recorded a half step lower.

Rap Lyrics

Rap 1: All right!
Stop what you're doing
'Cause I'm about to ruin
The image and the style that ya used to
I look funny
But yo I'm makin' money, see
So yo world I hope you're ready for me.
Now gather round
I'm the new fool in town
And my sound's laid down by the Underground
I drink up all the Hennessey ya got on ya shelf
So just let me introduce myself
My name is Humpty, pronounced with a Umpty.
Yo ladies, oh how I like to hump thee.
And all the rappers in the top ten
Please allow me to bump thee
I'm stepping tall, y'all
And just like Humpty Dumpty
You're gonna fall when the stereos pump me
I like to rhyme
I like my beats funky
I'm spunky, I like my oatmeal lumpy
I'm sick with this, straight gangsta Mac
But sometimes I get ridiculous
I'll eat up all your crackers and your licorice
Hey yo fat girl, come here, are you ticklish?
Yeah, I called you fat
Look at me, I'm skinny
It never stopped me from getting busy
I'm a freak
I like the girls with the boom
I once got busy in a Burger King bathroom
I'm crazy
Allow me to amaze thee
They say I'm ugly but it just don't faze me
I'm still gettin' in the girls' pants
And I even got my own dance

Rap 2: People say "Yo, Humpty, you're really funny looking"
That's all right 'cause I get things cookin'
You stare, you glare, you constantly try to compare me
But you can't get near me
I give 'em more, see, and on the floor, B,
All the girls they adore me
Oh yes, ladies, I'm really being sincere
'Cause in a 69 my Humpty nose will tickle your rear
My nose is big, uh-uh I'm not ashamed
Big like a pickle, I'm still getting paid
I get laid by the ladies, you know I'm in charge,
Both how I'm livin' and my nose is large
I get stoopid, I shoot an arrow like Cupid,
I use a word that don't mean nothing, like looptid
I sang on Doowhutchalike, and if ya missed it,
I'm the one who said just grab them in the biscuits
Also told you that I like to bite
Well, yeah, I guess it's obvious, I also like to write
All you had to do was give Humpty a chance
And now I'm gonna do my dance

Breakdown: Oh, yeah, that's the break, y'all
Let me hear a little bit of that bass groove right here
Oh, yeah!
Now that I told ya a little bit about myself
Let me tell ya a little bit about this dance
It's real easy to do - check it out

Rap 3: First I limp to the side like my leg was broken
Shaking and twitching kinda like I was smoking
Crazy whack funky
People say, "You look like M.C. Hammer on crack, Humpty."
That's all right 'cause my body's in motion
It's supposed to look like a fit or a convulsion
Anyone can play this game
This is my dance, y'all, Humpty Hump's my name
No two people will do it the same
You got it down when you appear to be in pain
Humping, funking, jumping
Jig around, shaking your rump
And when the dude a chump pump points a finger like a stump
Tell him step off, I'm doing the Hump

I WANNA SEX YOU UP

Words and Music by ELLIOT STRAITE,
BETTY WRIGHT and WILLIE CLARKE

Laid-back R&B feel

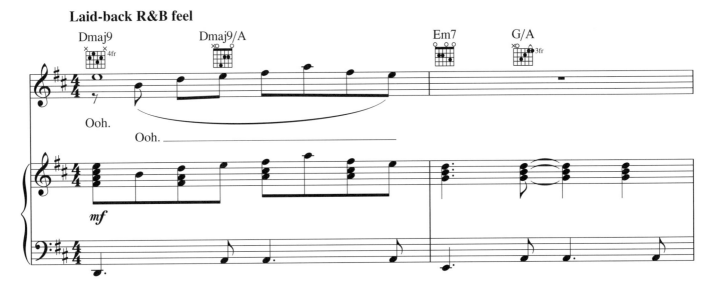

Ooh.
Ooh. _____

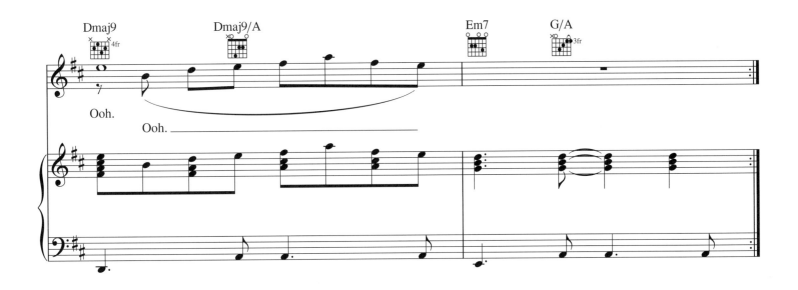

Ooh.
Ooh. _____

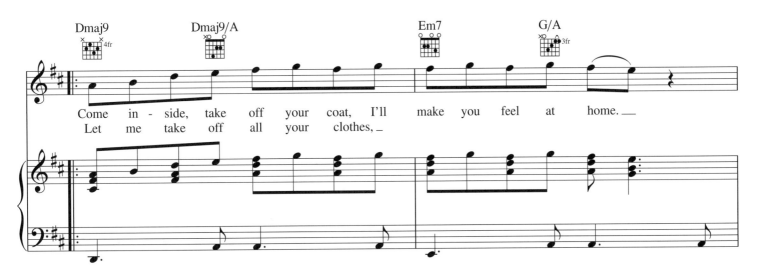

Come in- side, take off your coat, I'll make you feel at home. ___
Let me take off all your clothes, ___

I ALONE

Words and Music by EDWARD KOWALCZYK,
CHAD TAYLOR, PATRICK DAHLHEIMER
and CHAD GRACEY

Driving rock

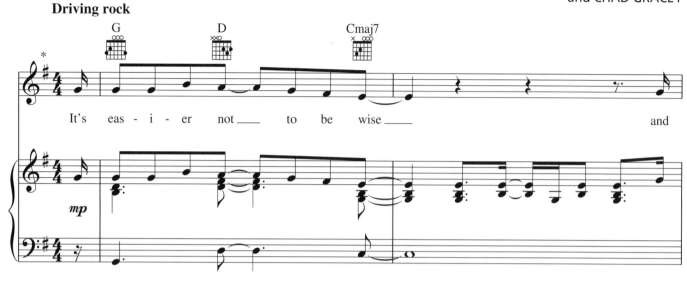

It's eas-i-er not___ to be wise___ and

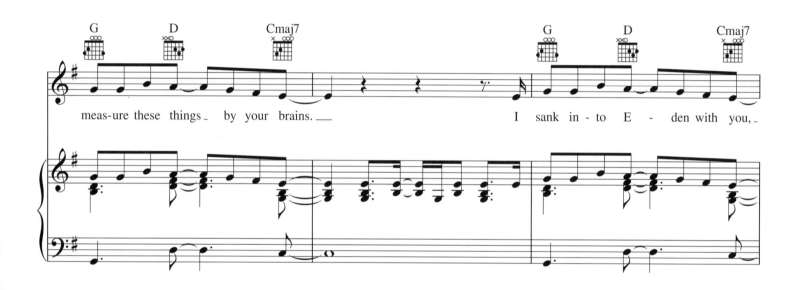

meas-ure these things__ by your brains.___ I sank in-to E - den with you,__

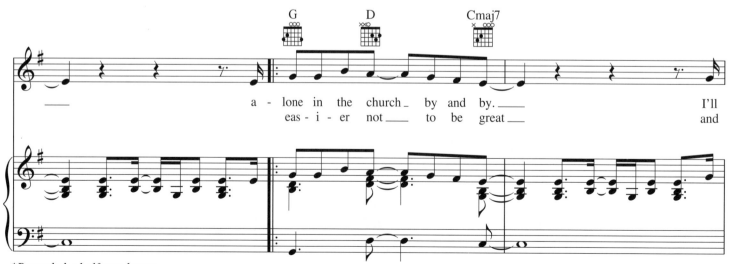

___ a - lone in the church__ by and by.___ I'll
eas - i - er not___ to be great___ and

*Recorded a half step lower.

Oh, now, we took it back __ too far, on-ly love __ can save __ us

now. ___ All these rid-dles that __ you burn, ___ all come run-ning back __ to

you. __ All these rhy-thms that __ you hide, ___ on-ly love __ can save __ us

D.S. al Coda

now, __ all these rid-dles that __ you burn, ___ yeah, yeah, yeah.

I DON'T WANT TO WAIT

Words and Music by
PAULA COLE

So o-pen up __ your morn-ing light __ and say a lit-tle prayer __ for I. __ You know that

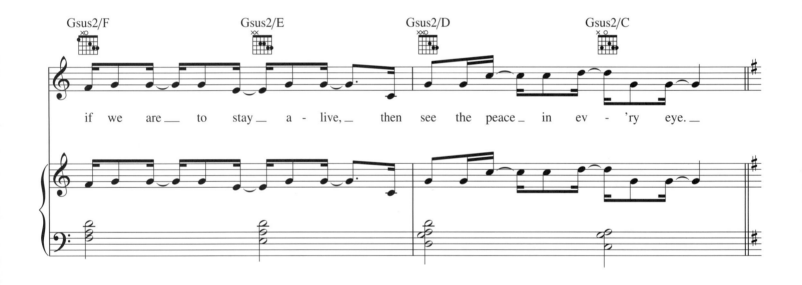

if we are __ to stay a-live, __ then see the peace __ in ev-'ry eye. __

Du du du __ du du, du du du __ du du,

Repeat and Fade

I WANT IT THAT WAY

Words and Music by MAX MARTIN
and ANDREAS CARLSSON

I WILL ALWAYS LOVE YOU
from THE BODYGUARD

Words and Music by
DOLLY PARTON

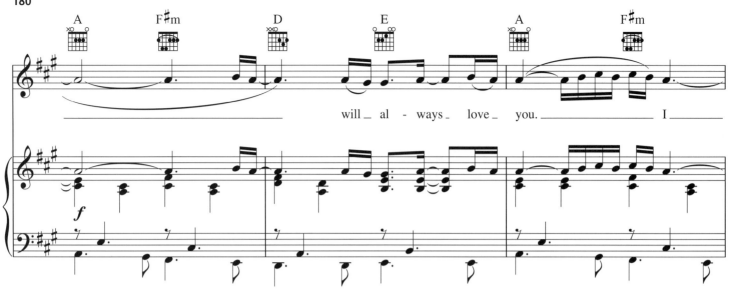

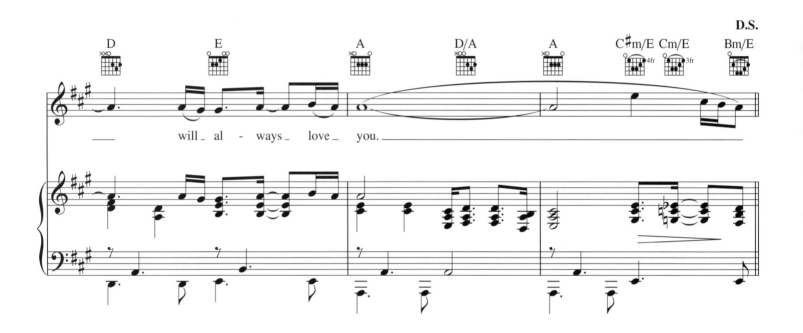

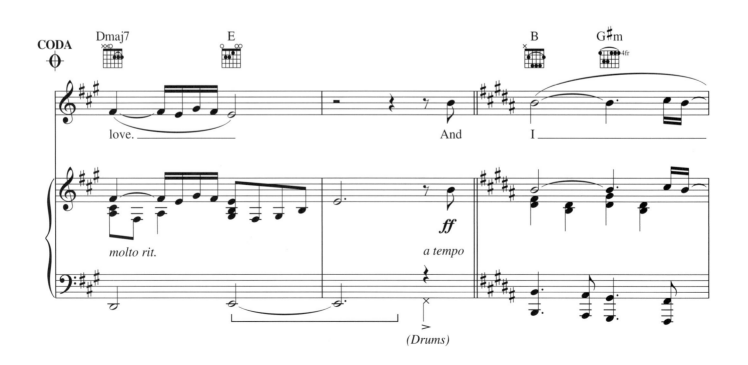

will al - ways love you. I will al - ways love

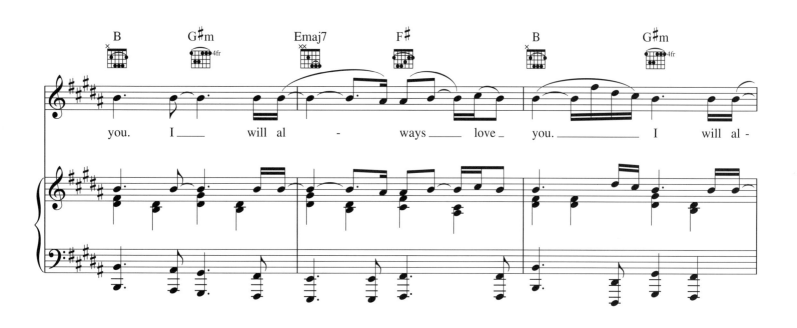

you. I will al - ways love you. I will al -

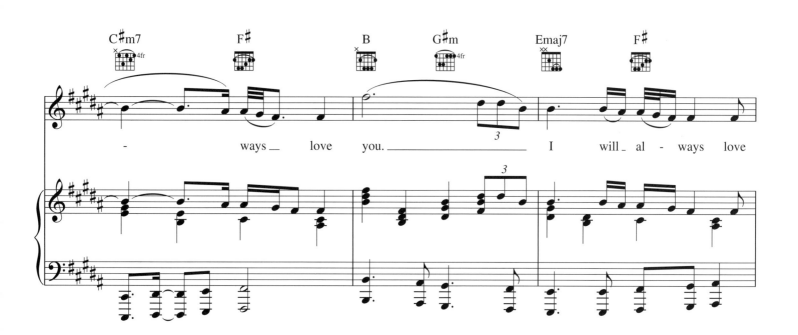

- ways love you. I will al - ways love

Additional Lyrics

3. I hope life treats you kind.
   And I hope you have all you've dreamed of.
   And I wish to you, joy and happiness.
   But above all this, I wish you love.

I'M TOO SEXY

Words and Music by RICHARD FAIRBRASS,
FRED FAIRBRASS and ROB MANZOLI

Moderate Dance beat

I'm too sex-y for my love, too sex-y for my love. Love's go-ing to leave

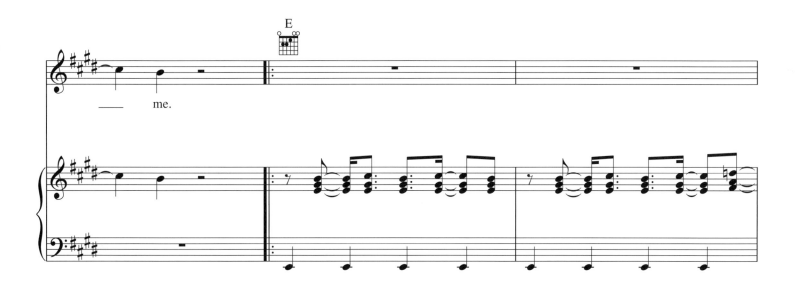

me.

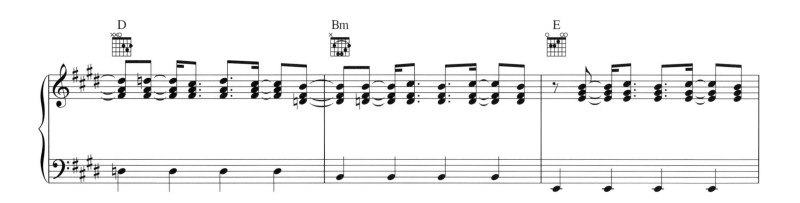

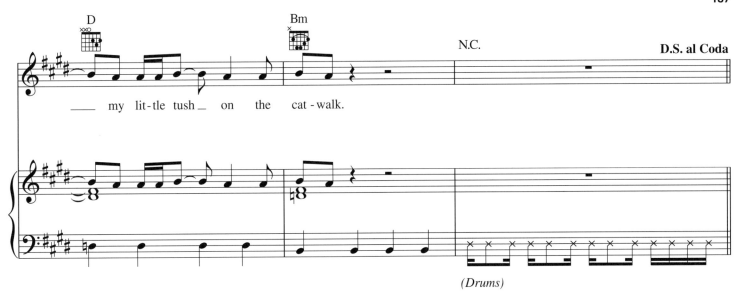

Additional Lyrics

2. I'm too sexy for my car, too sexy for my car,
   Too sexy by far.
   And I'm too sexy for my hat, too sexy for my hat.
   What d'ya think about that?
   Chorus

3. I'm too sexy for my cat, too sexy for my cat.
   Poor pussy, poor pussycat.
   I'm too sexy for my love, too sexy for my love.
   Love's going to leave me.
   Chorus

I'LL BE

Words and Music by
EDWIN McCAIN

The strands in your eyes ___ that col- or them ___

rain falls ___ an- gry on the

won- der- ful ___ stop me ___ and steal my ___ breath. ___

tin roof as ___ we lie ___ a- wake in my bed. ___

And em- 'ralds from moun- tains thrust towards the sky, ___

And you're my sur- viv- al, you're my liv- ing proof ___

* Recorded a half step lower.

ICE ICE BABY

Words and Music by VANILLA ICE,
EARTHQUAKE, M. SMOOTH, BRIAN MAY,
FREDDIE MERCURY, ROGER TAYLOR,
JOHN DEACON and DAVID BOWIE

Moderate Rap beat

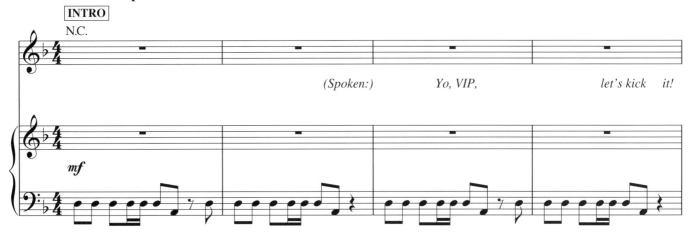

with **FIGURE A**

1. All right stop. Collaborate and listen
   Ice is back with my brand new invention
   Something grabs ahold of me tightly
   Then I flow like a harpoon daily and nightly
   Will it ever stop? Yo - I don't know
   Turn off the lights and I'll glow
   To the extreme I rock a mic like a vandal
   Light up a stage and wax a chump like a candle.

   Dance. Burn rush the speaker that booms
   I'm killing your brain like a poisonous mushroom
   Deadly, when I play a dope melody
   Anything less than the best is a felony
   Love it or leave it. You better gain way
   You better hit the bull's eye. The kid don't play
   If there was a problem, Yo, I'll solve it
   Check out the hook while my DJ revolves it

with **FIGURE A**

2. Now that the party is jumping
   With the bass kicked in, the Vegas are pumpin'
   Quick to the point, to the point no faking
   I'm cooking MC's like a pound of bacon
   Burning them if they're not quick and nimble
   I go crazy when I hear a cymbal
   And a hi hat with a souped up tempo
   I'm on a roll and it's time to go solo
   Rollin' in my 5.0
   With my ragtop down so my hair can blow
   The girlies on standby. Waving just to say Hi
   Did you stop? No - I just drove by
   Kept on pursuing to the next stop
   I busted a left and I'm heading to the next block
   That block was dead
   Yo - so I continued to A1A Beachfront Ave.

   Girls were hot wearing less than bikinis
   Rockman lovers driving Lamborghinis
   Jealous 'cause I'm out getting mine
   Shay with a guage and Vanilla with a nine
   Reading for the chumps on the wall
   The chumps acting ill because they're so full of eight balls
   Gunshots ranged out like a bell
   I grabbed my nine - All I heard were shells
   Falling on the concrete real fast
   Jumped in my car, slammed on the gas
   Bumper to bumper the avenue's packed
   I'm trying to get away before the jackers jack
   Police on the scene. You know what I mean
   They passed me up, confronted all the dope fiends
   If there was a problem, Yo, I'll solve it
   Check out the hook while my DJ revolves it

with **FIGURE B**

   Ice Ice Baby, Vanilla Ice Ice Baby
   Ice Ice Baby, Vanilla Ice Ice Baby

with **FIGURE A**

3. Take heed, 'cause I'm a lyrical poet
   Miami's on the scene just in case you didn't know it
   My town, that created all the bass sound
   Enough to shake and kick holes in the ground
   'Cause my style's like a chemical spill
   Feasible rhymes that you can vision and feel
   Conducted and formed, This is a hell of a concept
   We make it hype and you want to step with this
   Shay plays on the fade, slice like a ninja
   Cut like a razor blade so fast, Other DJ's say, "damn"
   If my rhyme was a drug, I'd sell it by the gram
   Keep my composure when it's time to get loose
   Magnetized by the mic while I kick my juice
   If there was a problem, Yo - I'll solve it!
   Check out the hook while Deshay revolves it.

with **FIGURE B**

   Ice Ice Baby, Vanilla Ice Ice Baby
   Ice Ice Baby, Vanilla Ice Ice Baby

with **FIGURE B**

Ice Ice Baby Too cold, Ice Ice Baby Too cold Too cold
Ice Ice Baby Too cold Too cold, Ice Ice Baby Too cold Too cold

INFORMER

Words and Music by SHAWN MOLTKE,
EDMOND LEARY, DARRIN O'BRIEN
and MICHAEL GRIER

Moderate Hip Hop

* Recorded a half step lower.

205

IT WAS A GOOD DAY

Words and Music by THE ISLEY BROTHERS,
CHRIS JASPER, ICE CUBE, A. GOODMAN,
S. ROBINSON and H. RAY

Laid-back Hip-Hop groove

Repeat as needed

Rap Lyrics

Rap 1: Just waking up in the morning, got to thank God
I don't know but today seems kinda odd
No barking from the dog, no smog
And Momma cooked a breakfast with no hog
I got my grub on, but didn't pig out
Finally got a call from a girl wanna dig out
Hooked it up on later as I hit the door
Thinking will I live, another twenty-four
I got to go cause I got me a drop top
And if I hit the switch, I can make the ass drop
Had to stop at a red light
Looking in my mirror not a jacker in sight
And everything is alright
I got a beep from Kim and she can fuck all night
Called up the homies and I'm askin y'all
Which court are y'all playin basketball?
Get me on the court and I'm trouble
Last week fucked around and got a triple double
Freaking niggers everyway like M.J.
I can't believe, today was a good day

Rap 2: Drove to the pad and hit the showers
Didn't even get no static from the cowards
'Cause just yesterday them fools tried to blast me
Saw the police and they rolled right past me
No flexing, didn't even look in a nigger's direction
As I ran the intersection
Went to Short Dog's house, they was watchin Yo! MTV Raps
What's the haps on the craps
Shake em up, shake em up, shake em up, shake em
Roll them in a circle of niggers and watch me break them
With the seven, seven-eleven, seven-eleven
Seven even back door little Joe
I picked up the cash flow
Then we played bones, and I'm yelling domino.
Plus nobody I know got killed in South Central L.A.
Today was a good day

Rap 3: Left my nigger's house paid
Picked up a girl been tryin to fuck since the twelfth grade
It's ironic, I had the brew she had the chronic
The Lakers beat the Supersonics
I felt on the big fat fanny
Pulled out the jammy, and killed the punanny
And my dick runs deep so deep so deep
Put her ass to sleep
Woke her up around one
She didn't hesitate, to call Ice Cube the top gun
Drove her to the pad and I'm coasting
Took another sip of the potion hit the three-wheel motion
I was glad everything had worked out
Dropped her ass off and then I chirped out
Today was like one of those fly dreams
Didn't even see a berry flashing those high beams
No helicopter looking for a murder
Two in the morning got the fat burger
Even saw the lights of the Goodyear blimp
And it read Ice Cube's a pimp
Drunk as hell but no throwing up
Half way home and my pager still blowing up
Today I didn't even have to use my A.K.
I got to say it was a good day

INSANE IN THE BRAIN

Words and Music by LARRY MUGGERUD,
LOUIS MARI FREESE and SENEN REYES

Moderate Hip-Hop groove

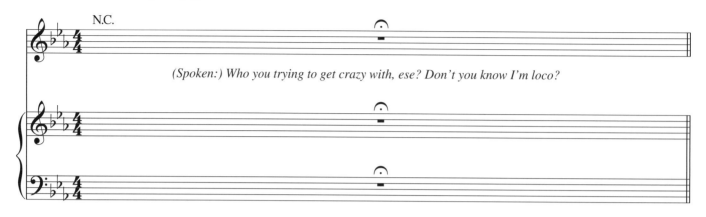

(Spoken:) Who you trying to get crazy with, ese? Don't you know I'm loco?

mf

Play 3 times for each verse

Rap 1-3. *(See rap lyrics)*

In - sane in the mem - brane, in - sane in the brain.

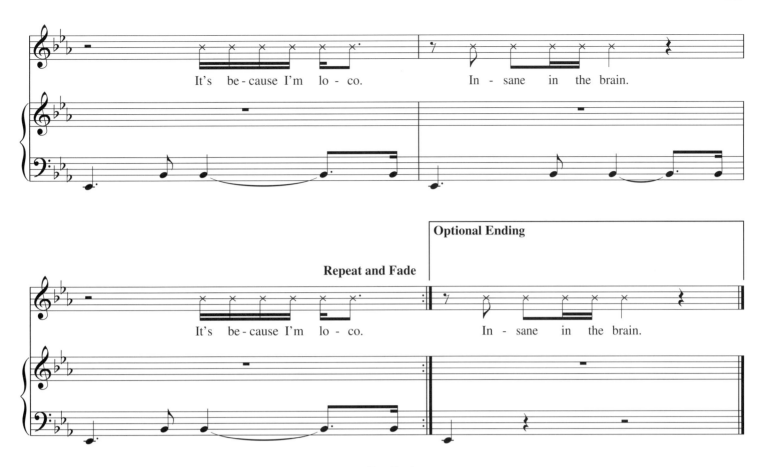

It's be-cause I'm lo - co.   In - sane in the brain.

Optional Ending

Repeat and Fade

It's be - cause I'm lo - co.   In - sane in the brain.

Rap Lyrics

Rap 1: To the one on the flam
Boy your temper just toss that ham
In the frying pan
Like spam
Feel done when I come in slam
Damn
I feel like the son of Sam
Don't make me wreck shit hectic
Next to the chair got me going like General Electric
Eeen!
The lights are blinking
I'm thinking
It's all over when I go out drinking
Oh, making my mind slow,
That's why I don't fuck with the big four O
Bro', I got to maintain
'Cause a nigger like me is going insane

Rap 2: Do my shit undercover
Now it's time for the blubba
Blabba
To watch that belly get fatter
Fat boy on a diet
Don't try it
I'll jack your ass like a looter in a riot
My shit's fat like a sumo slamming that ass
Leaving your face in the grass
You know I don't take a dulo
Lightly
Punks just jealous 'cause they can't outwrite me
So kick that style: wicked, wild
Happy face nigger never seen me smile
Rip that mainframe
I'll explain
A nigger like me is going insane

Rap 3: Like Louie Armstrong
Played the trumpet
I'll hit that bong and break you off something soon
I got to get my props
Cops
Come and try to snatch my crops
These pigs want to blow my house down
Head underground
To the next town
They get mad
When they come to raid my pad
And I'm out in the nine deuce Cad
Yes I'm the pirate pilot
Of this ship if I get
With the ultraviolet dream
Hide from the red light beam
Now do you believe in the unseen
Look, but don't make your eyes strain
A nigger like me is going insane

IRIS
from the Motion Picture CITY OF ANGELS

Words and Music by
JOHN RZEZNIK

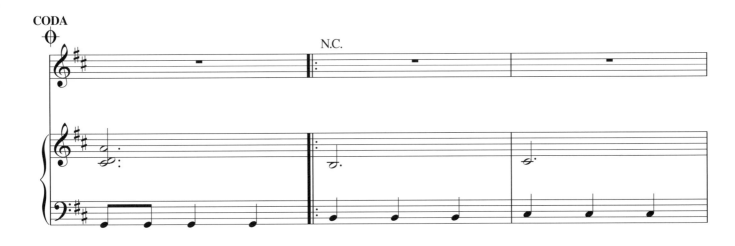

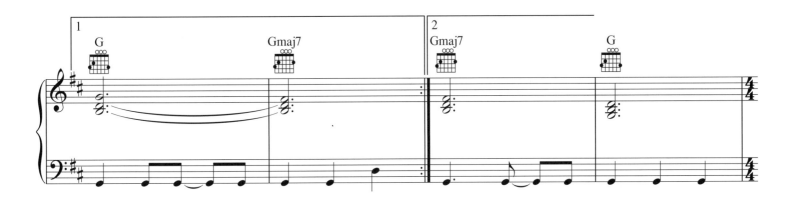

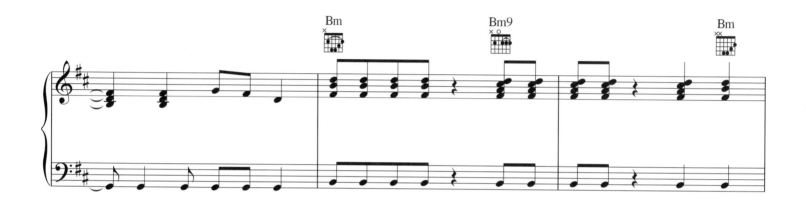

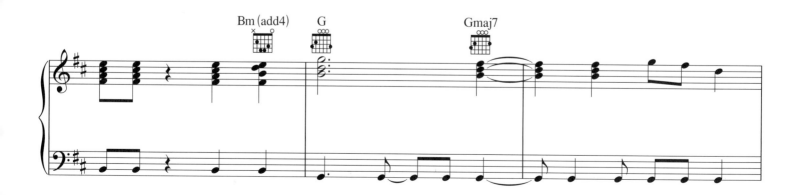

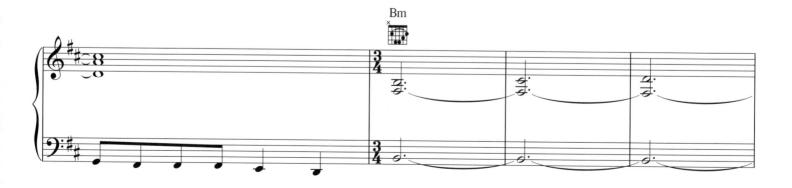

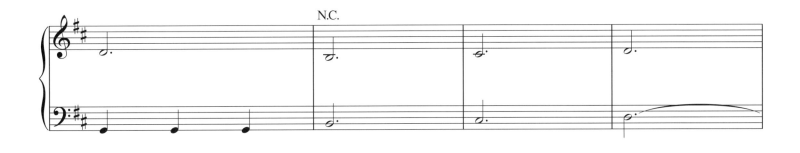

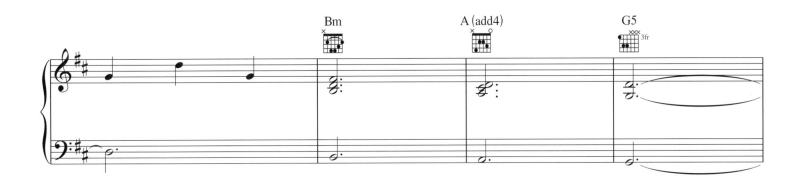

And I _____ don't want the world _____ to see _____ me

JEREMY

Music by JEFF AMENT
Lyric by EDDIE VEDDER

JUMP

Words and Music by FREDDIE PERREN, ALPHONSO MIZELL,
BERRY GORDY, DENNIS LUSSIER, JERMAINE DUPRI,
GREGORY WEBSTER, MELVIN PIERCE, NORMAN NAPIER,
ANDREW NOLAND, LEROY BONNER, MARSHALL JONES,
RALPH MIDDLEBROOKS and WALTER MORRISON

Moderate Rap

Kris Kross will not be having anything today. So as we

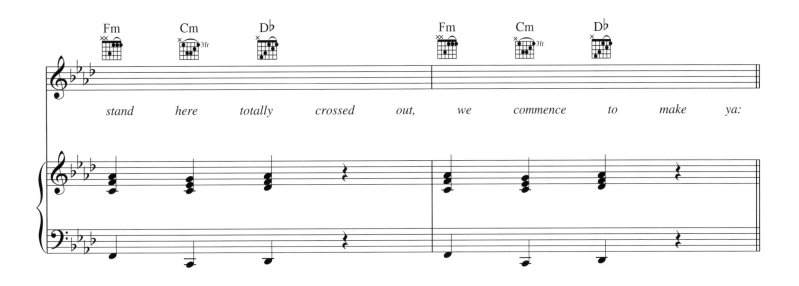

stand here totally crossed out, we commence to make ya:

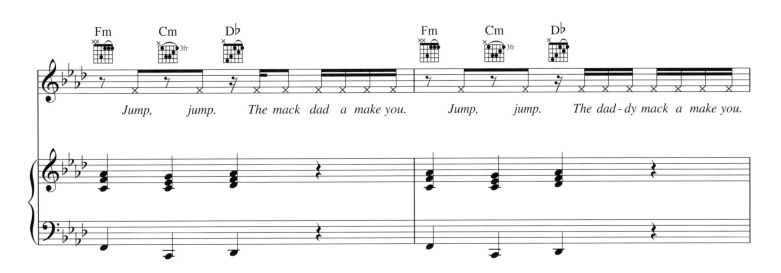

Jump, jump. The mack dad a make you. Jump, jump. The dad-dy mack a make you.

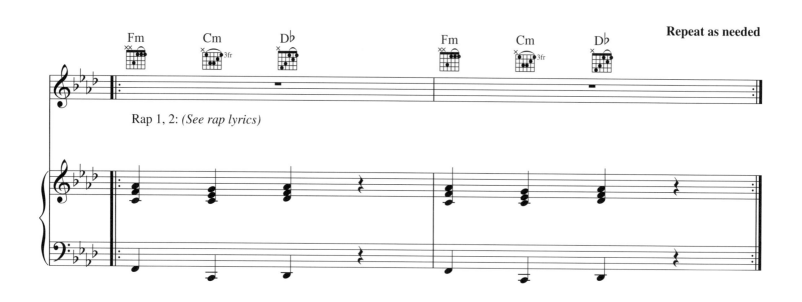

Jump, jump. Kris Kross ___ a make you. Jump, jump. Uh-huh, ah-huh. Jump, jump.

Rap Lyrics

Rap 1: Don't try to compare us 2 another bad little fad
I'm the mack and I'm bad
Given you something you never had
I make you bump, bump, wiggle and
Shake your rump
'Cause I be kickin' da flavor that makes
You wanna "Jump"

How high, real high
'Cause I'm just so fly
A young lovable, huggable
Type a guy
Everything is to the back
With a little slack
'Cause inside out is wigada,
Wigada, wigada, "Wack"

I come stumpin' with something pumpin'
To keep you jumpin'
R & B rappin' bull crap
Is what I'm dumpin'
Ain't nothing soft about Kris Kross
We all dat
So when they ask do they rock
Say believe dat
Chorus

Rap 2: I like my stuff knockin' "Knockin"
I love it when da girlies
Be like jockin', "Jockin'"
The D.A. double D.Y. M.A.C.
Yeah you know me
I got you jumpin' and bumpin' and pumpin'
Movin' all around "Gee"
I make the six step back
They dry to step to the mack
Then they got jacked
To the back you be sportin' your gear
Is that coincidental
"Act like you know and don't be claiming that it's mental"

Two li'l kids with a flow
You ain't never heard
Ain't nuttin' faking
You can understand every word
As you listen
To the smooth, smooth melody
The daddy makes you J.U.M.P.
Chorus

JUMP AROUND

Words and Music by LARRY E. MUGGERUD,
ERIK SCHRODY, BOB RELF,
EARL NELSON, FRED SMITH,
JIMMY WEBB and CHARLIE CRONANDER

With grandeur, freely

Moderate Hip-Hop groove

Rap 1,2: *(See rap lyrics)*

1, 2, 4, 5

3, 6

came to get down, _ I came to get down, _ so get out your seat and jump a - round. Jump a -

round. Jump a - round. Jump a -

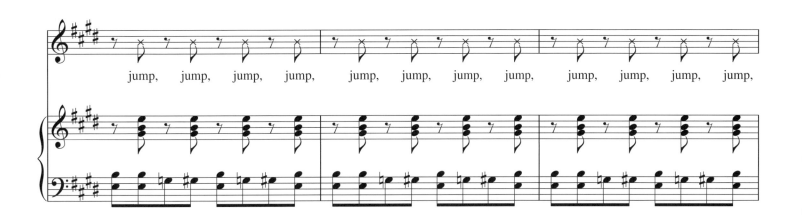

round. Jump up, jump up __ and get down. Jump,

jump, jump, jump, jump, jump, jump, jump, jump, jump, jump, jump, jump,

(Spoken:) This is dedicated to Joe 'Da Flava' Dakota. Grab your bosac, punk.

Rap Lyrics

Rap 1: Pack it up, pack it in
Let me begin, I came to win
Battle me that's a sin
I won't tear the sack up
Punk, you'd better back up
Try and play the role and the whole crew will act up
Get up, stand up, come on!
Come on, throw your hands up
If you've got the feeling, jump across the ceiling
Muggs is a funk fest, someone's talking junk
Yo, I'll bust them in the eye
And then I'll take the punks home
Feel it, funk it, amps it are junking
And I got more rhymes than there's cops that are dunking
Donuts shop
Sure enough I got props from the kids on the Hill
Plus my mom and my pops

Rap 2: I'll serve your ass like John McEnroe
If your steps up, I'm smacking the ho
Word to your moms, I came to drop bombs
I got more rhymes than the Bible's got psalms
And just like the prodigal son, I've returned
Anyone stepping to me, you'll get burned
Cause I got lyrics and you ain't got none
So if you come to battle bring a shotgun
But if you do you're a fool, cause I duel to the death
Try and step to me, you'll take your last breath
I got the skill, come get your fill
Cause when I shoot to give, I shoot to kill

Rap 3: I'm the cream of the crop, I rise to the top
I never eat a pig cause a pig is a cop
Or better yet a terminator
Like Arnold Schwarzenegger
Trying to play me out like as if my name was Sega
But I ain't going out like no punk bitch
Get used to one style and you know I might switch
It up, up and around, then buck, buck you down
Put out your head then you wake up in the Dawn of the Dead
I'm coming to get you, coming to get you
Spitting out lyrics, homie, I'll wet you

KILLING ME SOFTLY
WITH HIS SONG

Words by NORMAN GIMBEL
Music by CHARLES FOX

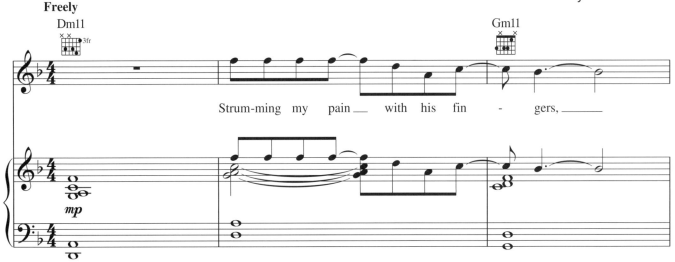

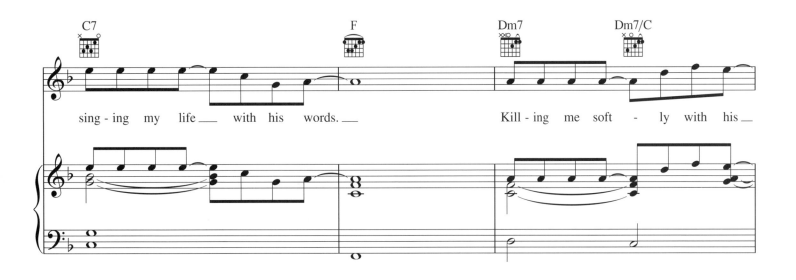

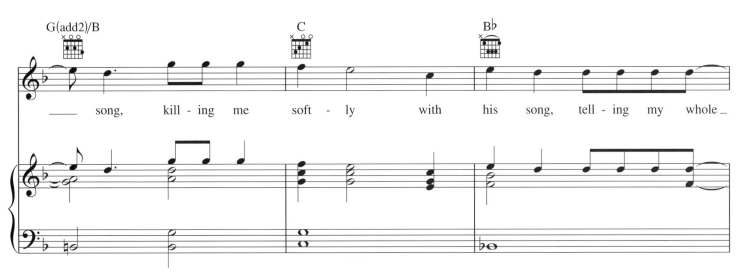

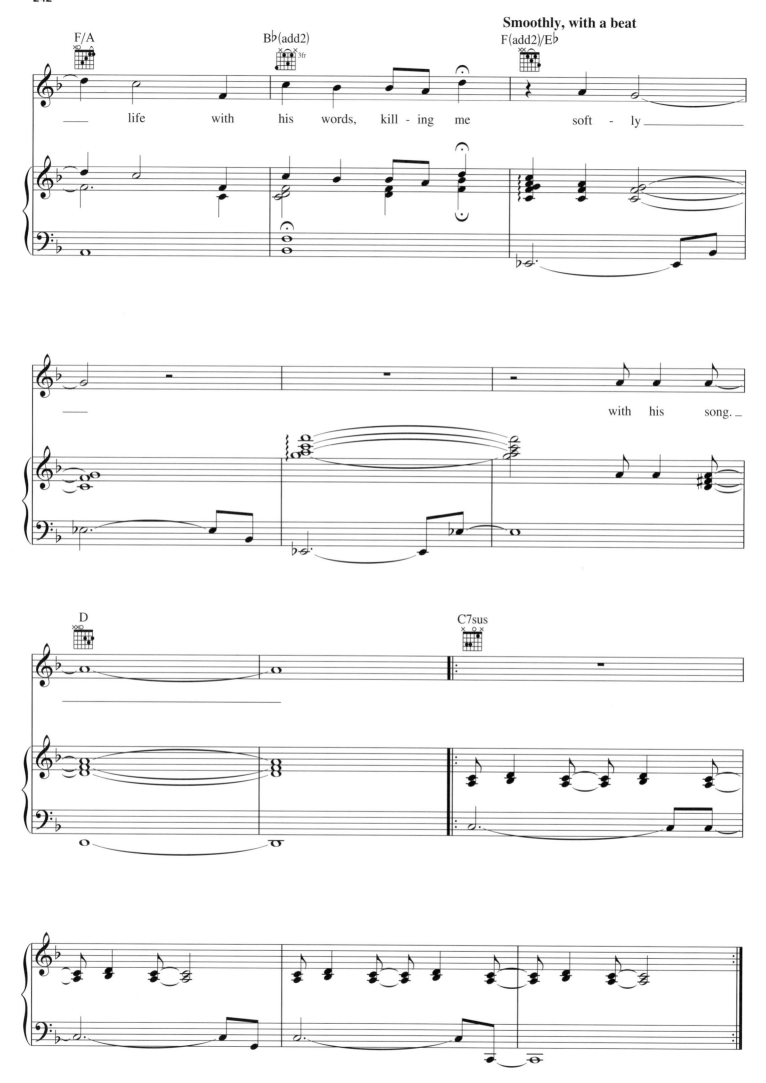

LIVIN' LA VIDA LOCA

Words and Music by ROBI ROSA
and DESMOND CHILD

She's in - to su - per - sti - tions, black cats and

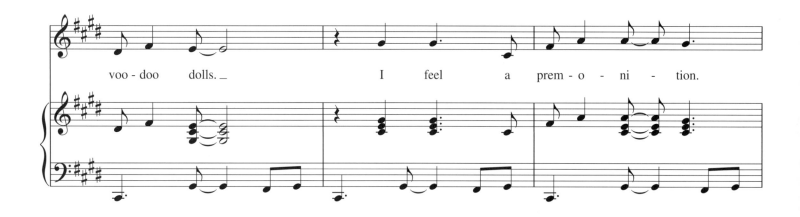

voo - doo dolls. ___ I feel a prem - o - ni - tion.

That girl's gon - na make me fall. ___

LOSER

Words by BECK HANSEN
Music by BECK HANSEN and KARL STEPHENSON

Moderately, not too fast

Rap 1: *(See rap lyrics)*

Soy un per - di - dor. I'm a

Repeat and Fade

los - er, ba - by. So, why don't you kill me?

Rap Lyrics

Rap 1: In the time of chimpanzees, I was a monkey
Butane in my veins and a mouth to cut the junkies with the plastic eyeballs.
Spray paint the vegetables. Dog food skulls with the beefcake pantyhose.
Kill the headlights and put it in neutral.
Got a couple of couches Stockcar flaming with the loser and the cruise control.
Baby's in Reno with the vitamin D. Got a couple of couches
Asleep on the love seat.
Someone keeps saying I'm insane to complain about a shotgun wedding
And a stain on my shirt.
Don't believe everything that you breathe.
You get a parking violation and a maggot on your sleeve.
So shave your face with some mace in the dark
Saving all your food stamps and burning down the trailer park.
Bent all the music with the phony gas chamber.
Yo, cut it.
Chorus

Rap 2: Forces of evil and a bozo nightmare.
'Cause one's got a weasel and another's got a flag.
One's on the pole. Shove the other in a bag with the rerun shows
And the cocaine nose job, the daytime crap of the folk singer slob.
He hung himself with guitar string.
A slab of turkey neck and it's hangin' from a pigeon wing.
So get right if you can't relate. Trade the cash for the beef
For the body for the hate.
And my time is a piece of wax falling on a termite
Who's choking on the splinters.
Chorus

LINGER

Lyrics by DOLORES O'RIORDAN
Music by DOLORES O'RIORDAN and NOEL HOGAN

LOSING MY RELIGION

Words and Music by BILL BERRY,
PETER BUCK, MIKE MILLS
and MICHAEL STIPE

(Can't Live Without Your)
LOVE AND AFFECTION

Words and Music by MARC TANNER,
MATT NELSON and GUNNAR NELSON

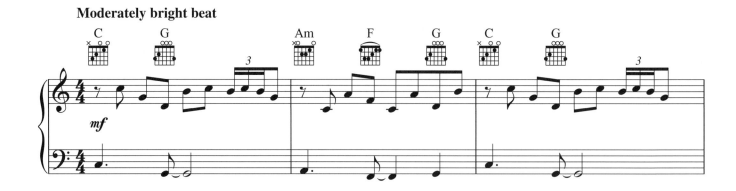

Here ____ she comes,   mm, ____
goes.   No,
wait,   mm, ____

____ just like an an - gel. ____ Seems like for - ev - er that she's
she don't know what she's miss - ing. Can't ____ she see I'll nev - er
____ here for an an - swer. Won - der if to - mor - row will be

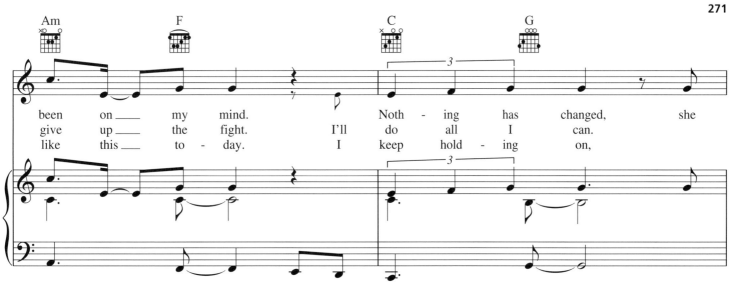

been on ___ my mind.
give up ___ the fight.
like this ___ to - day.

Noth - ing has changed, she
I'll do all I can.
I keep hold - ing on,

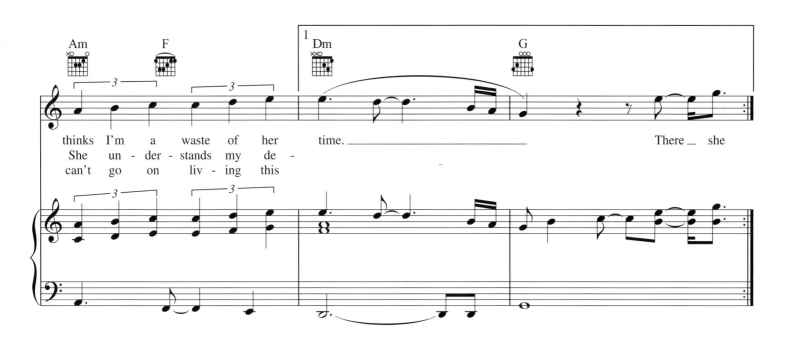

thinks I'm a waste of her time. ___
She un - der - stands my de -
can't go on liv - ing this

There ___ she

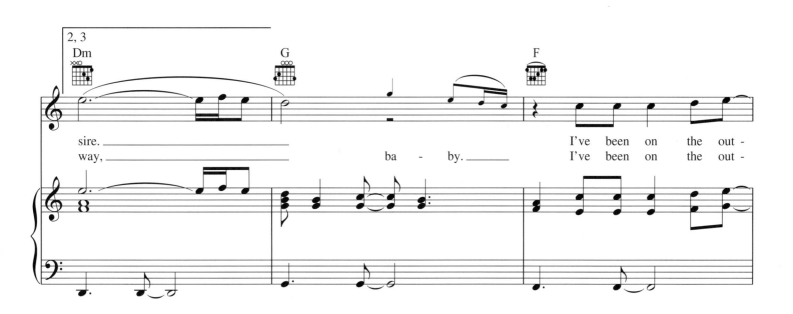

sire. ___
way, ___

ba - by. ___

I've been on the out -
I've been on the out -

With your   love, _____   I put my arms   a - round_ you.

MAMA SAID KNOCK YOU OUT

Words and Music by MARLON WILLIAMS,
WILLIAM COLLINS, JAMES SMITH, SYLVESTER STEWART,
GREGORY JACOBS, LEROY McCANTS, JAMES McCANTS,
GEORGE CLINTON and WALTER MORRISON

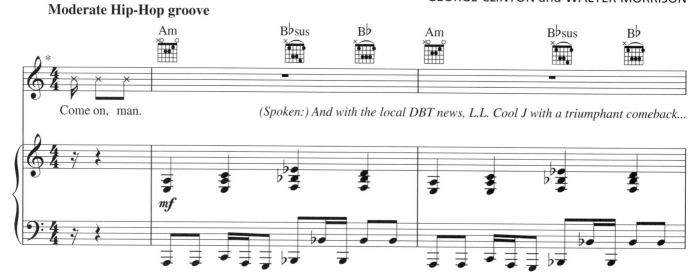

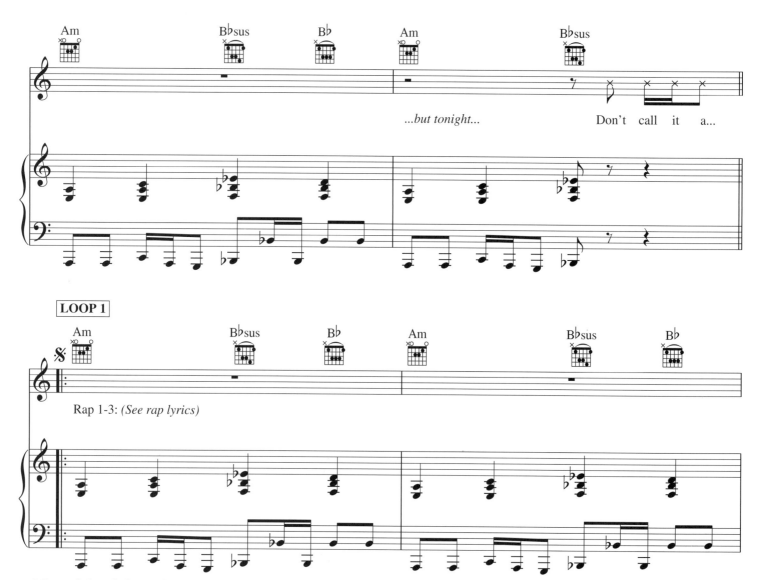

* *Recorded a whole step lower.*

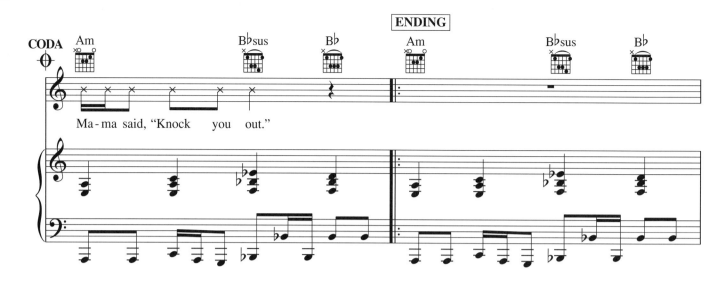

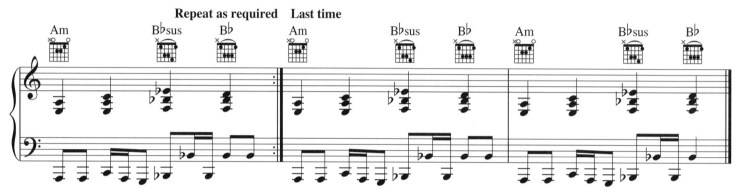

Rap Lyrics

Rap 1: Don't call it a comeback
(Loop 1) I been here for years
Rocking my peers and putting suckas in fear
Making the tears rain down like a monsoon
Listen to the bass go boom!
Explosion, overpowering
Over the competition, I'm towering
Wrecking shop, when I drop these lyrics that'll
Make you call the cops
Don't you dare stare, you better move
Don't ever compare
Me to the rest that'll all get sliced and diced
Competition's paying the price

Rap 2: Don't you call this a regular jam
(Loop 1) I'm gonna rock this land
I'm gonna take this itty bitty world by storm
And I'm just getting warm
Just like Muhummad Ali they called him Cassius
Watch me bash this beat like a skull
Cuz u know I had beef with
Why do u riff with me, the maniac psycho
And when I pull out my jammy get ready cuz it might go
Blaaaw, how you like me now?
The river will not allow
You to get with, Mr. Smith, don't riff
Listen to my gear shift
I'm blasting, outlasting
Kinda like Shaft, so you could say I'm shafting
Old English filled my mind
And I came up with a funky rhyme

Bridge: Shadow boxing when I heard you on the radio
I just don't know
What made you forget that I was raw?
But now I got a new tour
I'm going insane, starting the hurricane, releasing pain
Letting you know that you can't gain, I maintain
Unless ya say my name
Ripping, killing
Digging and drilling a hole
Pass the Old Gold

Rap 3: Shotgun blasts are heard
(Loop 1) When I rip and kill, at will
The man of the hour, tower of power, I'll devour
I'm gonna tie you up and let you understand
That I'm not your average man
When I got a jammy in my hand
Damn! Ooh!!
Listen to the way I slaaaaay, your crew
Damage, damage, damage, damage
Destruction, terror and mayhem
Pass me a sissy so suckas I'll slay him
Farmers (What?) Farmers (What?)
I'm ready (we're ready!)
I think I'm gonna bomb a town (get down!!)
Don't you never, ever, pull my lever
'Cause I explode
And my nine is easy to load
I got to thank God
'Cause he gave me the strength to rock
Hard, knock you out, Mama said, "Knock you out."

MIND PLAYING TRICKS ON ME

Words and Music by ISAAC HAYES,
BRAD JORDAN, WILLIE DENNIS
and DOUG KING

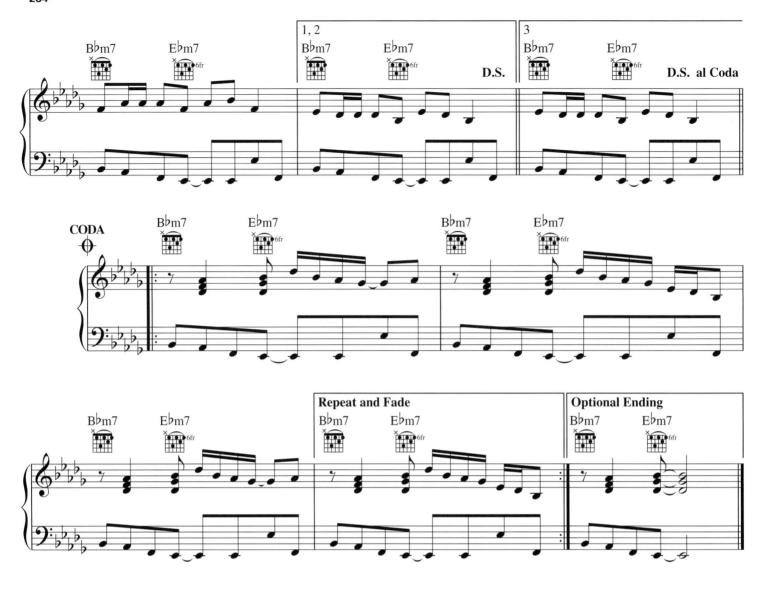

Rap Lyrics

Rap 1: At night I can't sleep, I toss and turn
(Loop) Candlesticks in the dark, visions of bodies bein' burned
Four walls just staring at a nigger
I'm paranoid, sleepin with my finger on the trigger
My mother's always stressing I ain't living right
But I ain't going out without a fight
See, everytime my eyes close
I start sweating, and blood starts coming out my nose
It's somebody watchin' the Ak
But I don't know who it is, so I'm watching my back
I can see him when I'm deep in the covers
When I awake I don't see the motherfucker
He owns a black hat like I own
A black suit and a cane like my own
Some might say, "Take a chill, B"
But fuck that shit! There's a nigger trying to kill me
I'm popping in the clip when the wind blows
Every twenty seconds got me peeping out my window
Investigating the joint for traps
Checking my telephone for taps
I'm staring at the woman on the corner
It's fucked up when your mind is playin' tricks on you

Rap 2: I make big money, I drive big cars
(Loop) Everybody know me, it's like I'm a movie star
But late at night, something ain't right
I feel I'm being tailed by the same sucker's headlights
Is it that fool that I ran off the block?
Or is it that nigger last week that I shot?
Or is it the one I beat for five thousand dollars
Thought he had 'caine but it was Gold Medal Flour
Reach under my seat, grabbed my popper for the suckers
Ain't no use to be lying, I was scareder than a motherfucker
Hooked a left into Popeye's and bailed out quick
If it's going down let's get this shit over with
Here they come, just like I figured
I got my hand on the motherfucking trigger
What I saw'll make your ass start giggling
Three black, crippled and crazy senior citizens
I live by the sword
I take my boys everywhere I go, because I'm paranoid
I keep looking over my shoulder and peeping around corners
My mind is playing tricks on me

Rap 3: Day by day it's more impossible to cope
(Loop) I feel like I'm the one that's doing dope
Can't keep a steady hand because I'm nervous
Every Sunday morning I'm in service
Praying for forgiveness
And trying to find an exit out the business
I know the Lord is looking at me
But yet it still is hard for me to feel happy
I often drift when I drive
Having fatal thoughts of suicide
Bang, and get it over with
And then I'm worry-free, but that's bullshit
I got a little boy to look after
And if I died then my child would be a bastard
I had a woman down with me
But to me it seemed like she was down to get me
She helped me out in this shit
But to me she was just another bitch
Now she's back with her mother
Now I'm realizing that I love her
Now I'm feeling lonely
My mind is playing tricks on me

Rap 4: This year Halloween fell on a weekend
(Loop) Me and Geto Boys are trick-or-treating
Robbing little kids for bags
Till an old man got behind our ass
So we speeded up the pace
Took a look back, and he was right before our face
He'd be in for a squabble no doubt
So I swung and hit the nigger in his mouth
He was going down, we figured
But this wasn't no ordinary nigger
He stood about six or seven feet
Now, that's the nigger I'd be seeing in my sleep
So we triple-teamed on him
Dropping them motherfucking B's on him
The more I swung the more blood flew
Then he disappeared and my boys disappeared, too
Then I felt just like a fiend
It wasn't even close to Halloween
It was dark as fuck on the streets
My hands were all bloody, from punching on the concrete
God damn, homie
My mind is playing tricks on me

MAN IN THE BOX

Written by JERRY CANTRELL, LAYNE STALEY,
SEAN KINNEY and MICHAEL STARR

Moderate Rock

Da da da da da da da da da da.

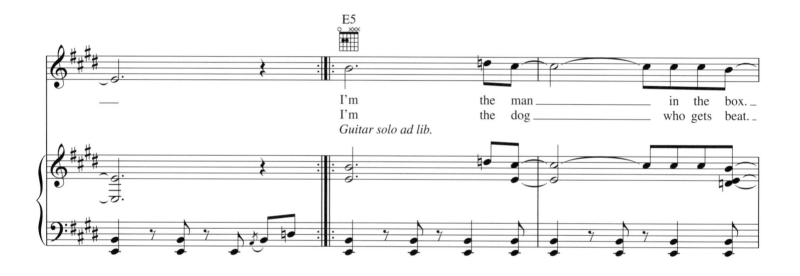

I'm the man in the box.
I'm the dog who gets beat.
Guitar solo ad lib.

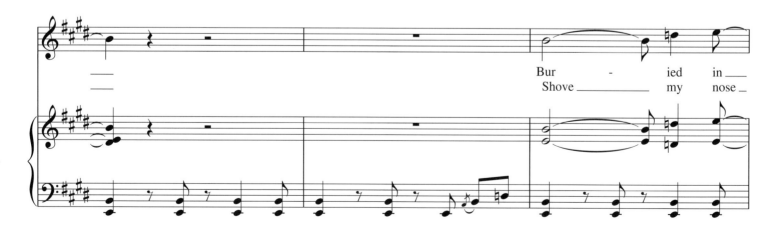

Bur - ied in
Shove my nose

MO' MONEY MO' PROBLEMS

Words and Music by SEAN "PUFFY" COMBS,
NOTORIOUS B.I.G., STEVEN JORDAN
and JASON PHILLIPS

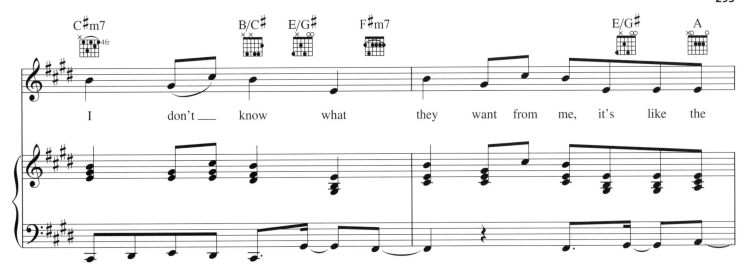

I don't ___ know what they want from me, it's like the

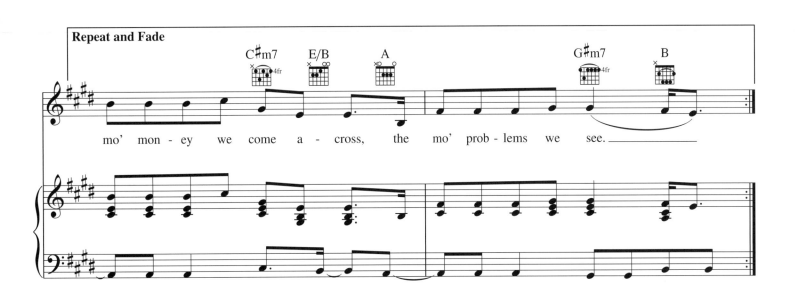

Repeat and Fade

mo' mon - ey we come a - cross, the mo' prob - lems we see. ___

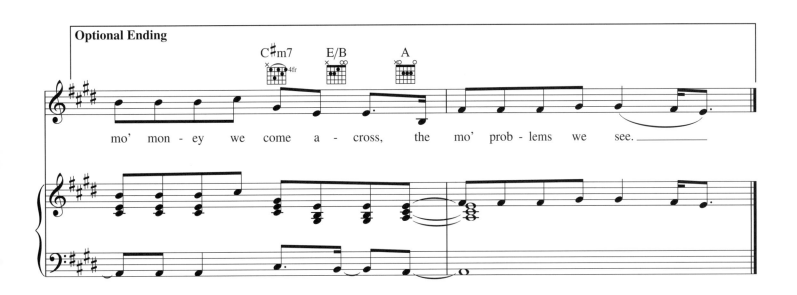

Optional Ending

mo' mon - ey we come a - cross, the mo' prob - lems we see. ___

Rap Lyrics

Rap 1: Now, who's hot who not
Tell me who rock who sell out in the stores
You tell me who flopped who copped the blue drop
Who jewels got robbed who's mostly Goldie down
To the tube sock, the same old pimp
Mase, you know ain't nothing change but my limp
Can't stop till I see my name on a blimp
Guarantee a million sales pullin' all the love
You don't believe in Harlem World nigga double up
We don't play around it's a bet lay it down
Nigga didn't know me ninety-one bet they know me now
I'm the young Harlem nigga with the Goldie sound
Can't no Ph.D. niggas hold me down, Cooter
Schooled me to the game, now I know my duty
Stay humble stay low blow like Hootie
True pimp niggas spend no dough on the booty
And then you yell there go Mase, there go your cutie.

Rap 2: From the C to the A to the D-D-Y
Know you'd rather see me die than to see me fly
I call all the shots
Rip all the spots, rock all the rocks
Cop all the drops, I know you thinking now's
When all the ballin' stops, nigga never home
Got to call me on the yacht
Ten years from now we'll still be on top
Yo, I thought I told you that we won't stop
Now whatcha gonna do when it's cool
Bag of money much longer than yours
And a team much stronger than yours, violate me
This'll be your day, we don't play
Mess around be D.O.A., be on your way
'Cause it ain't enough time here, ain't enough lime here
For you to shine here, deal with many women
But treat dimes fair, and I'm
Bigger than the city lights down in Times Square.

Rap 3: B.I.G. P-O-P-P-A
No info, for the DEA
Federal agents mad cause I'm flagrant
Tap my cell, and the phone in the basement
My team supreme, stay clean
Triple beam lyrical dream, I be that
Cat you see at all events bent
Gats in holsters girls on shoulders
Playboy, I told ya, bein' nice to me
Bruise too much, I lose, too much
Step on stage the girls boo too much
I guess it's 'cause you run with lame dudes too much
Me lose my touch, never that
If I did, ain't no problem to get the gat
Where the true players at?
Throw your Rollies in the sky
Wave 'em side to side and keep your hands high
While I give your girl the eye, player please
Lyrically, niggas see, B.I.G.
Be flossin' jig on the cover of *Fortune*
Five double oh, here's my phone number
Your man ain't got to know, I got to go
Got the flow down phzat, platinum plus
Like thizat, dangerous
On trizack, leave your ass blizack.

MY LOVIN'

Words and Music by THOMAS McELROY
and DENZIL FOSTER

MR. JONES

Words by ADAM DURITZ
Music by ADAM DURITZ and DAVID BRYSON

MY HEART WILL GO ON
(Love Theme from 'Titanic')
from the Paramount and Twentieth Century Fox Motion Picture TITANIC

Music by JAMES HORNER
Lyric by WILL JENNINGS

MY NAME IS

Words and Music by
LABI SIFFRE

Moderately slow

Hi, my name is... What? My name is... Who? My name is Slim Shad - y.

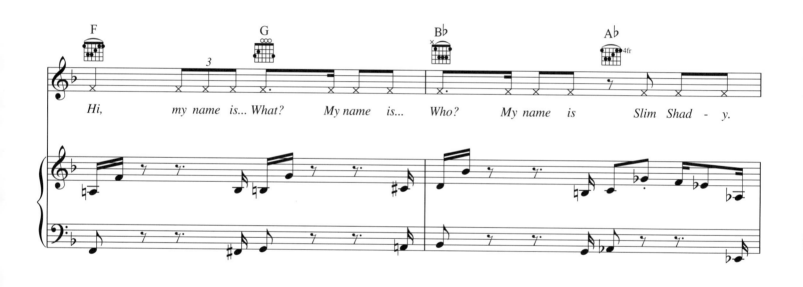

Hi, my name is... What? My name is... Who? My name is Slim Shad - y.

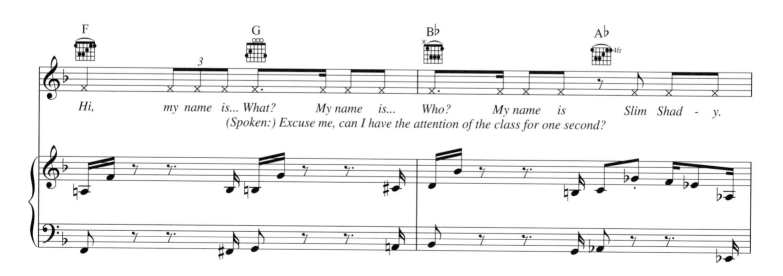

Hi, my name is... What? My name is... Who? My name is Slim Shad - y.
(Spoken:) Excuse me, can I have the attention of the class for one second?

Chorus

Repeat ad lib. and Fade

Rap Lyrics

Rap 1: Hi, kids! Do you like Primus?
Wanna see me stick nine-inch nails
Through each one of my eyelids?
Wanna copy me and do exactly like I did?
Try 'cid and get *****-up worse than my life is?
My brain's dead weight.
I'm trying to get my head straight,
But I can't figure out which Spice Girl I wanna impregnate.
And Dr. Dre said, "Slim Shady, you're perverted."
I know, but, "Just watch your mouth.
This is the clean version."
Well, since age twelve, I felt like a caged elf
Who stayed to himself in one place chasing this tail.
Got ticked-off and ripped Pamela Lee's lips off,
Kissed 'em and said,
"I ain't know silicone was supposed to be this soft."
I'm 'bout to pass out and crash and fall in the grass,
Faster than a fat man who sat down too fast.
Come here, lady!
"Shady, wait a minute, that's my girl dog."
I don't give a damn,
Dre sent me to tick the world off.
Chorus

Rap 2: My English teacher wanted to flunk me in junior high,
Thanks a lot. Next semester, I'll be thirty-five.
I smacked him in his face with an eraser,
Chased him with a stapler,
And told him to change the grade on the paper.
Walked into the strip club, had my jacket zipped up.
Flashed the bartender and stuck my **** in her tip cup.
Extraterrestrial running over pedestrians in a spaceship
While they're screaming at me, "Let's just be friends."
Ninety-nine percent of my life, I was lied to.
I just found out my mom does more **** than I do.
I told her I'd grow up to be a famous rapper,
Make a record about doin' ***** and name it after her.
You know you blew up when the women rush the stage
And try to touch your hands like some screaming Usher fans.
This guy at White Castle asked me for my autograph,
So I signed it, "Dear Dave, thanks for the support, *******!"
Chorus

Rap 3: Stop the tape, this kid needs to be locked away.
Get him!
Dr. Dre, don't just stand there... operate!
I'm not ready to leave, it's too scary to die.
I'd rather be carried inside the cemetery and buried alive.
Am I coming or going? I can barely decide.
I just drank a fifth of Coolade; dare me to drive?
Go ahead. All of my life I was very deprived.
I ain't had a woman in years
And my palms are too hairy to hide.
Clothes ripped like The Incredible Hulk.
I spit when I talk, I **** anything that walks.
Come here!
When I was little, I used to get so hungrya I would throw fits.
"How you gonna breast-feed me, Mom, you ain't got to ****?"
I lay awake and strap myself in the bed,
With a bulletproof vest on and tapped myself in the head,
'Cause I'm steamin' mad.
And by the way, when you see my dad,
Ask him if he brought a porno mag and seen my ad.
Chorus

NEVER SAID

Words and Music by
LIZ PHAIR

*Melody is written an octave higher than sung.

911 IS A JOKE

Words and Music by WILLIAM COLLINS,
KEITH BOXLEY, ERIC SADLER, GEORGE CLINTON,
BERNARD WORRELL and WILLIAM DRAYTON

Chorus

So get up, __ get, get, get __ down. Nine-one-one is a joke __ in your __ town.

To Coda ⊕

Get up, __ get, get, get __ down. Late nine-one-one wears the late __ crown.

D.S. al Coda

Optional Ending

Repeat ad lib. and Fade

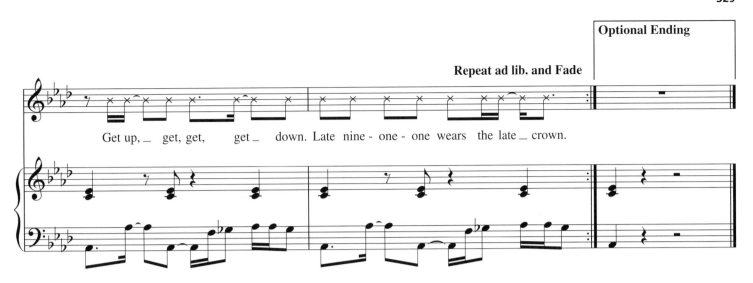

Get up, __ get, get, get __ down. Late nine - one - one wears the late __ crown.

Rap Lyrics

Rap 1: Now I dialed 911 a long time ago
Don't you see how late they're reacting
They only come and they come when they want to
So get the morgue truck, and embalm the goner
They don't care 'cause they stay paid anyway
They teach you like an ace they can't be betrayed
I know you stumble with no use people
If your life is on the line then you're dead today
Late comings with the late coming stretcher
That's a body bag in disguise y'all betcha
I call them body snatchers quick they come to fetch you?
With an autopsy ambulance just to dissect you
They are the kings 'cause they swing amputation
Lose your arms, your legs to them it's compilation
I can prove it to you watch the rotation
It all adds up to a funky situation.
Chorus

Rap 2: Every day they don't never come correct
You can ask my man right here with the broken neck
He's a witness to the job never being done
He would've been in full in 8 9-11
Was a joke 'cause they always joking
They the token to your life when it's croaking
They need to be in a pawn shop on a
911 is a joke we don't want them
I call a cab 'cause a cab will come quicker
The doctors huddle up and call a flea flicker
The reason that I say that 'cause they
Flick you off like fleas
They be laughing at you while you're crawling on your knees
And to the strength so go the length
Thinking you are first when you really are tenth
You better wake up and smell the real flavor
'Cause 911 is a fake lifesaver.
Chorus

NO DIGGITY

Words and Music by CHAUNCEY HANNIBAL,
EDWARD RILEY, WILLIAM STEWART,
RICHARD VICK, LYNISE WALTERS
and BILL WITHERS

Rap Lyrics

Rap 1: It's goin' down, fade to Blackstreet.
The homies got RB collab' creations.
Bump like acne, no doubt.
I put it down, never slouch.
As long as my credit could vouch,
A dog couldn't catch me staying out, and tell me,
Who could stop with Dre makin' moves,
Attractin' honeys like a magnet,
Giving them eargasms with my mellow accent
Still movin' his flavour
With the homies Blackstreet and Teddy,
The original rump shakers.

Rap 2: Cuz, that's my peeps and we rows D,
Flyin' first class from New York City to Blackstreet.
What you know about me? Not a motherfucking thing.
Cartier wooded frames sported by my shorty.
As for me, icy gleam and pinky diamond ring.
We be's the baddest clique up on this scene.
Ain't you gettin' bored with these fake ass broads?
High shows and proves, no doubt, I be diggin' you.
So please excuse, if I come across rude.
That's just me and that's how a playette's got to be.
Stay kickin' game with a capital G.
Ask the peoples on my block, I'm as real as can be.
Word is born, fakin' moves never been my thing.
So, Teddy, pass the word to your nigga Chauncy,
I'll be sendin' a car, let's say around 3:30.
Queen Pen and Blackstreet, it's no diggity.

Additional Lyrics

Verse 2: She's got class and style,
Street knowledge by the pound.
Baby never act wild,
Very low key on the profile.
Catchin' villains is a no.
Let me tell you how it goes.
Curve's the word, spin's the verb,
Lovers it curves so freak what you heard.
Rollin' with the fatness,
You don't even know what the half is.
You got to pay to play
Just for shorty, bang bang, to look your way.
I like the way you work it,
Trump tight, all day, ev'ry day.
You're blowin' my mind, maybe in time,
Baby, I can get you in my ride.

O.P.P.

Words and Music by ALPHONSO MIZELL,
FREDDIE PERREN, DENNIS LUSSIER, BERRY GORDY,
ANTHONY CRISS, KEIR GIST and VINCENT BROWN

Rap 1: O.P.P.: how can I explain it?
I'll take you frame by frame it.
To have y'all jumpin', shall we singin' it.
O is for "other," P is for "people," scratchin' temple.
The last P, well, that's not that simple, huh.
It's sorta like a, well, another way to call a cat a kitten.
It's five letters that are missin' here.
You get it on occasion at the other party as a game,
An' it seems I gotta start the explainin'. Bust it.
You ever had a girl and met her on a nice hello?
You get her name and number, then you feelin' real mellow.
You get home, wait a day; she's what you wanna know about.
Then you call up and it's her girlfriend's or her cousin's house.
It's not a fronter, F to the R to the O to the N to the T.
It's just her boyfriend's at her house. (Oh, that's what is scary.)
It's O.P.P. time, other people's what you get it.
There's no room for relationship, there's just room to hit it.
How many brothers out there know just what I'm gettin' at?
Who thinks it's wrong 'cause I was splittin' and co-hittin' at?
Well, if you do, that's O.P.P., and you're not down with it,
But if you don't, here's your membership.

Rap 2: As for the ladies, O.P.P. means something gifted.
The first two letters are same, but the last is something different.
It's the longest, loveliest, lean—I call it the leanest.
It's another five letter word rhymin' with cleanest and meanest.
I won't get into that; I'll do it, uh, sorta properly.
I say the last P...hmm...stands for "property."
Now, lady, here comes a kiss, blow a kiss back to me.
Now, tell me, exactly,
Have you ever known a brother who had another, like a girl or wife?
And you just had to stop and just 'cause he look just as nice.
You looked at him, he looked at you, and you knew right away
That he had someone, but he was gonna be yours anyway.
You couldn't be seen with him, and honestly, you didn't care
'Cause in a room behind a door, no one but y'all are there.
When y'all are finished, y'all can leave, and only y'all would know,
And y'all could throw that skeleton bone right in the closet door.
Now, don't be shocked, 'cause if you're down, I want your hands up high.
Say, "O.P.P." (O.P.P), I like to say with pride.
Now when you do it, do it well, and make sure that it counts.
You're now down with a discount.

Rap 3: This girl tried to O.P.P. me.
I had a girl, and she knew that, matter-of-fact, uh, my girl was partners
That had a fallout, disagreement, yeah, an argument.
She tried to do me so we did it in my apartment, bust it.
That wasn't the thing, it must have been the way she hit the ceiling,
'Cause after that, she kept on comin' back and catchin' feelings.
I said, "Let's go, my girl is comin', so you gotta leave."
She said, "Oh no, I love you, Treach."
I said, "Now, child, please,
You gots to leave, come grab your coat right now, you gotta go."
I said, "Now, look you to the stairs and to the stair window.
This was a thing, a little thing— you shouldn't have put your heart,
'Cause you know I was O.P.P, hell, from the very start."
Come on, come on, now let me tell you what it's all about.
When you get down, you can't go 'round runnin' off at the mouth.
That's rule number one in this O.P.P. establishment.
You keep your mouth shut and it won't get back to her or him.
Exciting, isn't it? A special kinda business.
Many of you will catch the same sorta O.P.P visit with
Him or her, for sure, are goin' to admit it.
When O.P.P comes, damn, skippy, I'm with it.

NOTHING COMPARES 2 U

Words and Music by
PRINCE

Oh. _____

All the flow - ers that you plant-ed, ma-ma, in the back yard _____

NUTHIN' BUT A G THANG

Words and Music by FREDERICK KNIGHT,
LEON HAYWOOD and CORDOZAR CALVIN BROADUS

Rap Lyrics

Rap 1: But uh, back to the lecture at hand,
Perfection is perfected so I'm a let them understand
From a young G's perspective.
And before me dig out a bitch I have to find a contraceptive.
You never know she could be earning her man
And learning her man, and at the same time burning her man
Now you know I ain't with that shit, Lieutenant
Ain't no pussy good enough to get burnt while I'm up in it
Now that's realer than real-deal Holyfield
And now all you hookers and ho's know how I feel
Well, if it's good enough to get broke off a proper chunk
I'll take a small piece of some of that funky stuff.

Rap 2: Well, I'm peeping, and I'm creeping, and I'm creep-in
But I damn near got caught, 'cause my beeper kept beeping
Now it's time for me to make my impression felt
So sit back, relax, and strap on your seatbelt
You never been on a ride like this before
With a producer who can rap and control the maestro
At the same time with the dope rhyme that I kick
You know, and I know, I flow some old funky shit
To add to my collection, the selection
Symbolizes dope, take a toke, but don't choke
If you do, you have no clue
Of what me and my homey Snoop Dogg came to do.

Rap 3: Falling back on that ass with a hellified gangsta lean
Getting funky on the mic like an old batch of collard greens
It's the capital S, oh yes, the fresh N-double-O-P
D-O-double-G-Y-D-O-double-G you see
Showing much flex when it's time to wreck a mic
Pimping ho's and clocking a grip like my name was Dolomite
Yeah, and it don't quit
I think they in a mood for some mothafucking G shit
So Dre. *(What up, Dogg?)*
We gotta give them what they want *(What's that, G?)*
We gotta break them off something *(Hell yeah)*
And it's gotta be bumping *(City of Compton!)*

Rap 4: It's where it takes place so I'm a ask your attention
Mobbing like a mothafucka but I ain't lynching
Dropping the funky shit that's making the sucker niggas mumble
When I'm on the mic, it's like a cookie, they all crumble
Try to get close, and your ass'll get smacked
My mothafucking homie Doggy Dogg has got my back
Never let me slip, 'cause if I slip, then I'm slipping
But if I got my neener, then you know I'm straight tripping
And I'm a continue to put the rap down, put the mack down
And if you bitches talk shit, I have to put the smack down
Yeah, and you don't stop
I told you I'm just like a clock when I tick and I tock
But I'm never off, always on, 'til the break of dawn
C-O-M-P-T-O-N, and the city they call Long Beach
Putting the shit together
Like my nigga D.O.C., no one can do it better.

ONE OF US

Words and Music by
ERIC BAZILIAN

ONE WEEK

Words and Music by
ED ROBERTSON

It -'ll still be two days till we __ say we're sor - ry.

Additional Lyrics

2. Chickity China the Chinese chicken,
   Have a drumstick and your brain stops tickin'.
   Watchin' X-Files with no lights on.
   We're *dans la maison*.
   I hope the Smoking Man's in this one.
   Like Harrison Ford, I'm getting frantic.
   Like Sting, I'm tantric.
   Like Snickers, guaranteed to satisfy.
   Like Kurasawa, I make mad films.
   OK, I don't make files,
   But if I did, they'd have a Samurai.
   Gonna get a set a' better clubs;
   Gonna find the kind with tiny nubs
   Just so my irons aren't always flying
   Off the backswing.
   Gotta get in tune with Sailor Moon,
   'Cause the cartoon has got
   The boom Anime babes
   That make me think the wrong thing.
   To Bridge

ONLY WANNA BE WITH YOU

Words and Music by DARIUS CARLOS RUCKER,
EVERETT DEAN FELBER, MARK WILLIAM BRYAN
and JAMES GEORGE SONEFELD

You and me, ___ we come from dif-f'rent worlds. ___

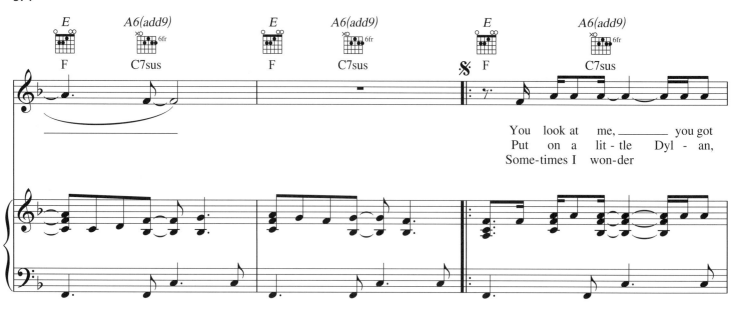

You look at me, _____ you got
Put on a lit-tle Dyl-an,
Some-times I won-der

noth-ing left ___ to say. ___
sit-ting on ___ a fence. ___
if it will ev-er end. ___

I moan and pout ___ at you ___ un-til
I say, "That line ___ is great." ___ You ask ___
You get so mad ___ at me when I go ___

___ I get ___ my ___ way.
___ me what ___ I meant by
___ out with ___ my ___ friends.

I won't dance, ___
"Said I shot a man ___ named Gray, ___
Some-times you're cra-zy

Peaches

Words and Music by CHRIS BALLEW,
DAVE DEDERER and JASON FINN

Moderate Rock, not too fast

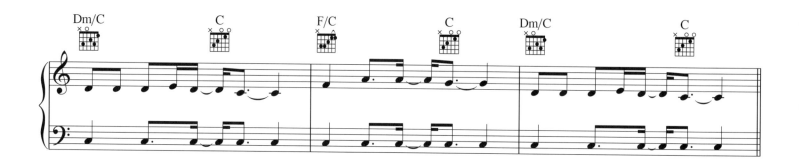

Mov-ing to the coun-try, ___ I'm gon-na eat a lot of peach-es. ___ I'm

mov-ing to the coun-try, ___ I'm gon-na eat me a lot of peach-es. ___ I'm

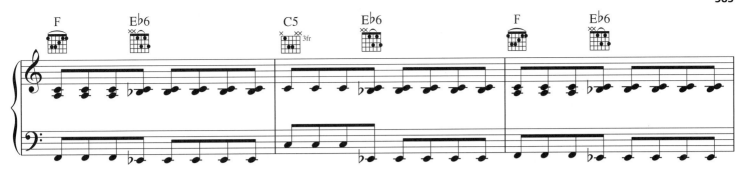

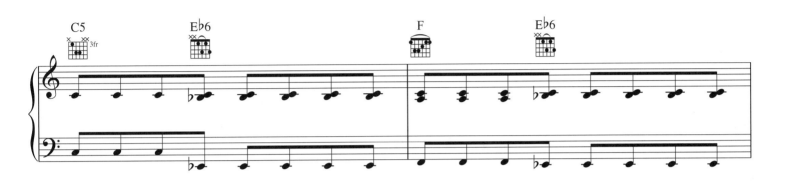

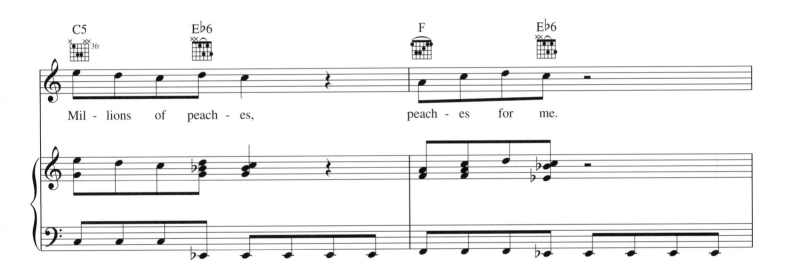

Mil - lions of peach - es, peach - es for me.

Mil - lions of peach - es, peach - es for free.

Mil - lions of peach - es, peach - es for me.

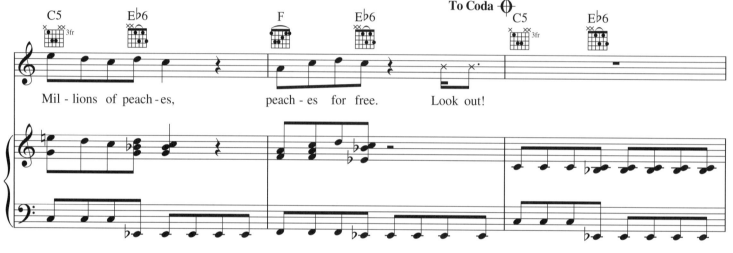

Mil - lions of peach - es, peach - es for free. Look out!

To Coda ⊕

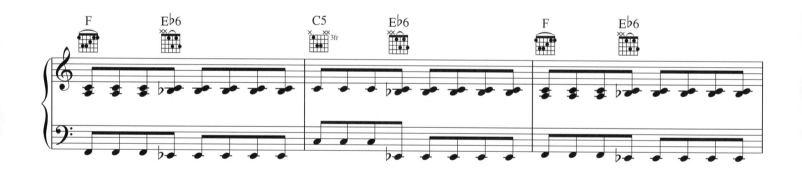

D.S. al Coda

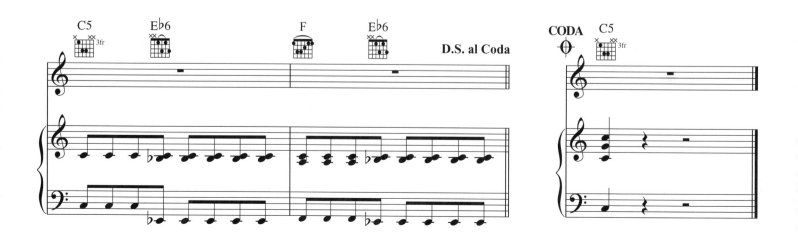

CODA ⊕

RICO SUAVE

Words and Music by GERARDO MEJIA,
CHRISTIAN CARLOS WARREN, ALBERTO SLEZYNGER
and ROSA SOY

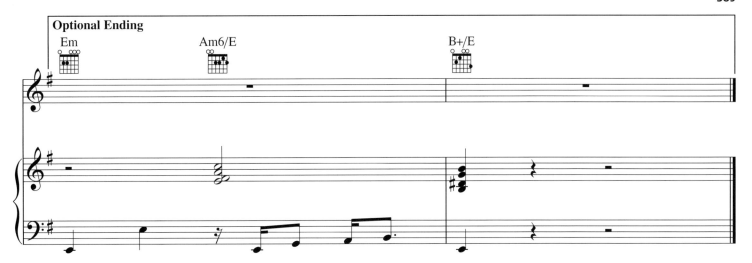

Rap Lyrics

Rap 1: Seguro que han oído que yo soy educado
Soy un caballerito un chico bien portado
Un joven responsible y siempre bien vestido
Yo no se quien ha mentido
I don't drink or smoke ain't into dope
Won't try no coke, ask me how I do it, I cope
My only addiction has to do with the female species
I eat them raw like sushi
No me gustan ternos, mi estilo es moderno
Si me enterno, you me enfermo
Mi apariencia es dura, vivo en la locura
No me vengan con ternuras
So please don't judge a book by its cover
There's more to being a Latin lover
You got to know how to deal with a woman
That won't let go
The price you pay for being a gigolo

Rap 2: There's not a woman that can handle a man like me
That's why I juggle two or three
I ain't one to commit, you can omit that bit
You pop the question that's it
Haber uno, dos, tres, cuatro mujeres
Y la situacíon alli no muere
No es un delito calmo mi apetito
Con un llanto o un grito
So again don't let my lyrics mislead you
I don't love you but I need you
Would you rather have me lie
Take a piece of your pie and say bye
Or be honest and rub your thighs?

Rap 3: Well, it's ten o'clock and I'm two hours late
I never said I was a prompt date
But you kept persisting that I meet your parents
Huh, they're going to love my appearance
Ding dong el timbre suena
Tu madre abre, que vieja mas buena
Le digo ¡Hola! Pero no para bola
Que se ha creido vieja chola
Go and serve the food mom
Que tengo ambre
If you don't hurry, me va a dar un calambre
Y usted señor? Why's your chin on the floor?
Sierra la boca por favor
What's this amor, these little huevos?
Esto si que yo no pruebo
I'm used to good ol' fashioned
Homestyle Spanish cooking
If I try that I'll be puking
Well it's been a pleasure but we got to go
Regresaremos temprano
Cinco, seis, o siete de la mañana
Su hija esta en buenas manos

THE RAIN
(Supa Dupa Fly)

Words and Music by ANN PEEBLES,
BERNARD MILLER, DON BRYANT,
MELISSA ELLIOT and TIMOTHY MOSLEY

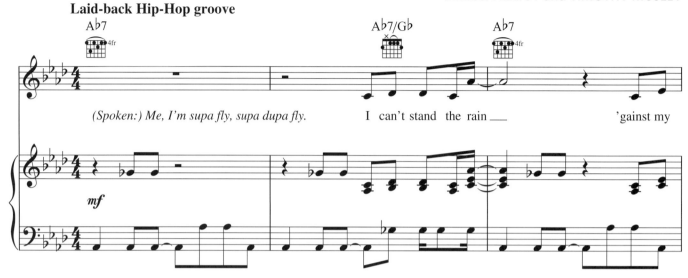

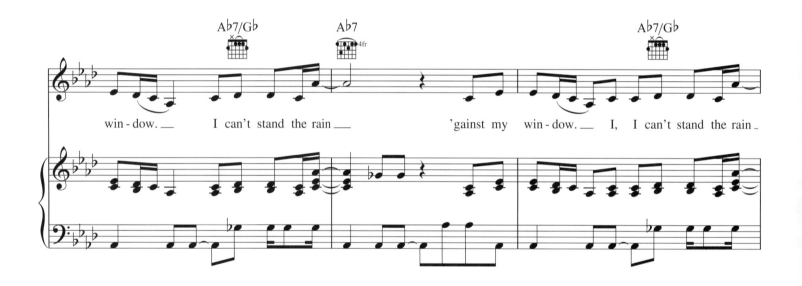

391

Rap Lyrics

Rap 1: When the rain hits my window
I take a puff, puff me some indo
Me and Timbaland, oh
We tango-dango
We so tight that you get our styles tangled
Sway-lo dosi-do like you loco
Can we get kinky tonight?
Like CoCo, so so
You don't wanna play with my yo-yo
I smoke my hydro on the D-lo

Rap 2: Beep Beep
Who got the keys to the jeep?
Vroom, I'm driving to the beach
Top down, loud sounds see my peeps
Give them pound, now look who it be
It be me me me and Timothy
Look like it's about to rain what a shame
I got the Armor All to shine up the stain
Oh Missy, try to maintain
Freaky freaky freaky

Rap 3: I feel the wind
Five six seven, eight nine ten
Begin, I sit on hills like Lauryn
Until the rain starts
Comin' down, pouring, chill
I got my umbrella
My finger waves these days
They fall like Humpty
Chunky, I break up with him before he dump me
To have me yes you lucky

RUN AROUND

Words and Music by
JOHN POPPER

things up when all it does is slow

me down?

Harmonica solo ad lib.

Repeat and Fade

Optional Ending

SABOTAGE

Words and Music by MICHAEL DIAMOND,
ADAM YAUCH and ADAM HOROVITZ

Fast Hard Rock

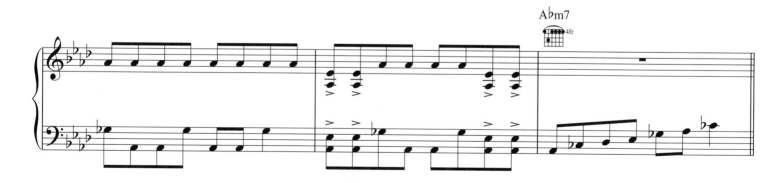

Rap 1, 4: (See rap lyrics)

To Coda ⊕
Play 4 times

Play 3 times

Rap 2: (See rap lyrics)

Play 2 times

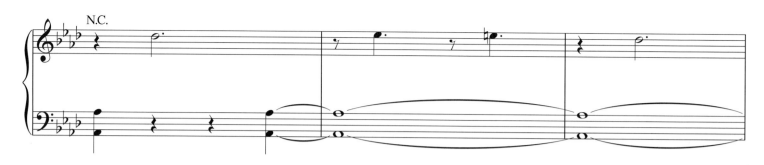

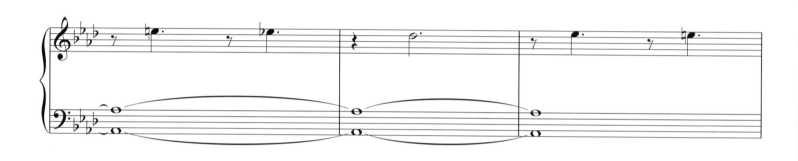

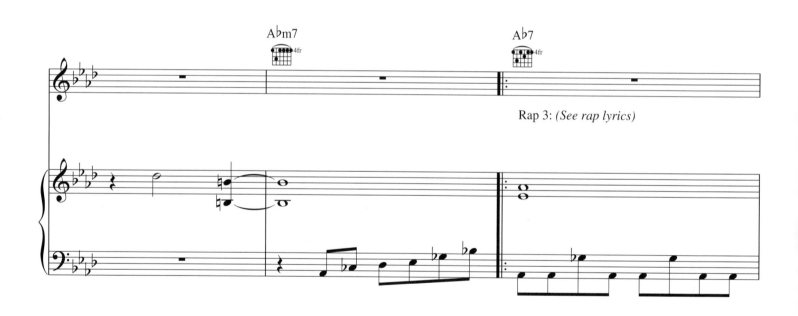

Rap 3: *(See rap lyrics)*

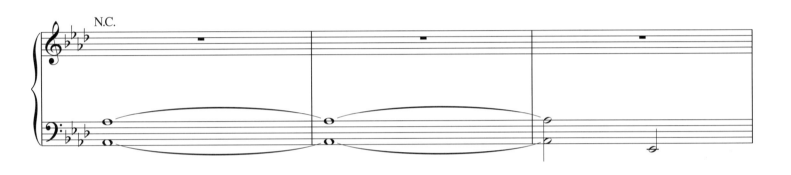

Rap Lyrics

Rap 1: I can't stand it. I know you planned it. I'm gon' set it straight, this Watergate.
I can't stand rockin' when I'm in here 'cause your crystal ball ain't so crystal clear.
So, while you sit back and wonder why, I got this fuckin' thorn in my side.
Oh my God, it's a mirage. I'm tellin' y'all it's sabotage.

Rap 2: So, so, so listen up 'cause you can't say nothin'. You shut me down with a push of your button.
Betcha I'm out and I'm gone. I'll tell you now I keep it on and on.

Rap 3: 'Cause what you see you might not get, and we can bet so don't you get souped yet.
Schemin' on a thing that's a mirage. I'm tryin' to tell you now it's sabotage.

Rap 4: I can't stand it. I know you planned it. I'm gon' set it straight, this Watergate.
But I can't stand rockin' when I'm in this place because I feel disgrace because you're all in my face.
But make no mistakes and switch up my channel. I'm Buddy Rich when I fly off the handle.
What could it be, it's a mirage. You're schemin' on a thing that's sabotage.

SAY MY NAME

Words and Music by RODNEY JERKINS,
LASHAWN DANIELS, FRED JERKINS,
BEYONCE KNOWLES, KELENDRIA ROWLAND,
LATAVIA ROBERSON and LETOYA LUCKETT

Cm ... **A♭**

know you say that I am as-sum-ing things. Some-thing's go-ing down, that's the way it seems. _

Fm ... **Fm7/B♭** ... **Bdim7**

Should-n't be no rea-son why you're act-ing strange _ if no-bod-y's hold-ing you back from me. _ 'Cause

Cm ... **A♭**

I know how you usual-ly do, _ where you're say-ing ev-'ry-thing to me times two.

Fm ... **Fm7/B♭** ... **Bdim7**

Why can't you just tell the truth? _ If some-bod-y's there, then tell me who. _

SEMI-CHARMED LIFE

Words and Music by
STEPHAN JENKINS

SEX AND CANDY

Words and Music by
JOHN WOZNIAK

Mellow Rock

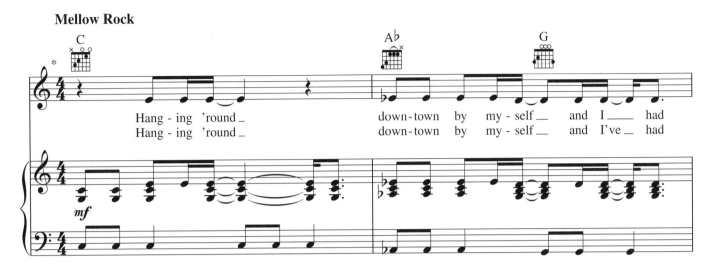

Hang - ing 'round _____ down-town by my - self _____ and I _____ had
Hang - ing 'round _____ down-town by my - self _____ and I've _____ had

so much time _____ to sit and think a - bout _____ my - self. _____ 'N'then there she was _____
too much caf - feine and I was think-ing 'bout _____ my - self. _____ 'N'then there she was _____

like dou - ble cher - ry pie, _____ yeah, there she was _____
in plat - form dou - ble suede, _____ yeah, there she was _____

Recorded a half step lower.

SHINE

Words and Music by
ED ROLAND

Moderate Rock

(1.,3.) Give me a word, give me a sign, show me where to look, tell me what will I
(2.) Love is in the water, love is in the air, show me where to look, tell me will love be

find, ___ what will I ___ find? ___
there, ___ will love be ___ there? ___

Recorded a half step higher.

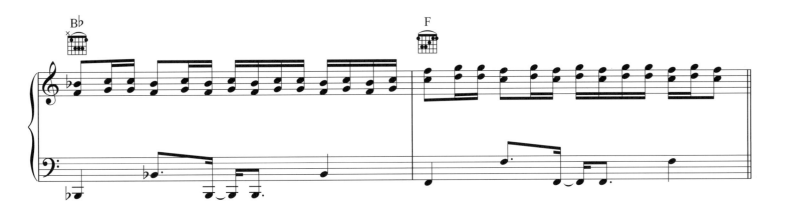

Double-time feel

Guitar solo

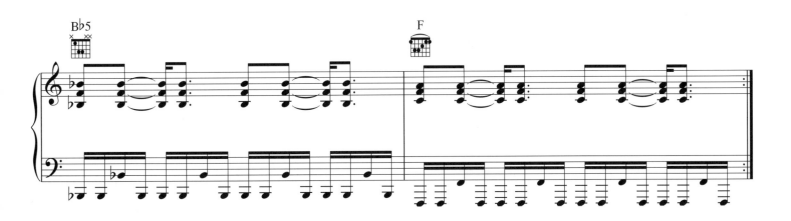

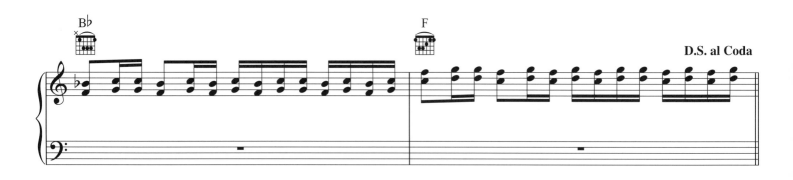

light shine __ down.   I'm gon-na   let it   shine, __ I'm gon-na let it   shine, __

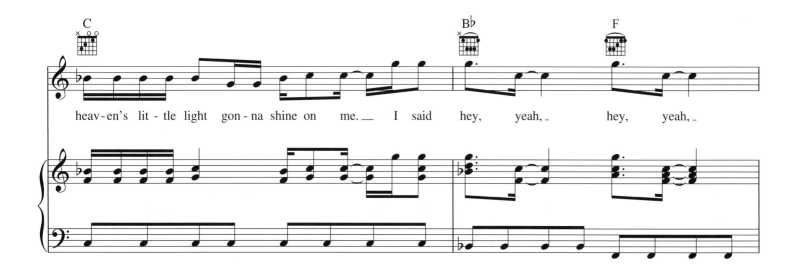

heav-en's lit-tle light gon-na shine on me. __ I said   hey,   yeah, __   hey,   yeah, __

SMELLS LIKE TEEN SPIRIT

Words and Music by KURT COBAIN,
KRIST NOVOSELIC and DAVE GROHL

A♭5 D♭5 F5 B♭5 A♭5 D♭5
4fr 4fr 4fr 4fr
-g'rous. Here we are now; en-ter-tain us. I feel stu-
F5 B♭5 A♭5 D♭5 F5 B♭5
4fr 4fr
-pid and con-ta-gious. Here we are now; en-ter-tain
A♭5 D♭5 F5 B♭5 A♭5 D♭5
4fr 4fr 4fr 4fr
To Coda
us. A mu-lat-to, an al-bi-no, a mos-qui-
F5 B♭5 A♭5 D♭5 F5 E5 F5 G♭5
4fr 4fr
N.C.
-to, my li-bi-do. Yeah! Oy.

TEARIN' UP MY HEART

Words and Music by MAX MARTIN
and KRISTIAN LUNDIN

It's tear-in' up my heart when I'm __ with you, __ but when we are a-

part I feel __ it, too. __ And no mat-ter what __ I __ do __

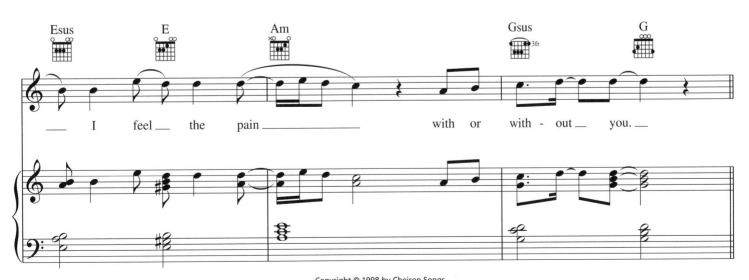

__ I feel __ the pain __ with or with-out __ you. __

STAY

Words and Music by
LISA LOEB

TENNESSEE

Words and Music by TODD THOMAS
and TARRE JONES

Moderately slow

1. Lord, I've real-ly been _ real stressed, _ down and out, los-ing ground.
2., 3. *(See additional lyrics)*

Al-though I am black _ and proud, _ prob-lems got me pes-si-mis-tic.

Broth-ers and sis-ters keep mess-in' up, _ why does it have to be so damn tuff?

* Recorded a half step lower.

Additional Lyrics

2. Lord, it's obvious we got a relationship
   Talkin' to each other every night and day
   Although You're superior over me
   We talk to each other in a friendship way
   Then outta nowhere You tell me to break
   Outta the country and into more country
   Past Dyesburg and Ripley
   Where the ghost of childhood haunts me
   Walk the roads my forefathers walked
   Climb the trees my forefathers hung from
   Ask those trees for all their wisdom
   They tell me my ears are so young.*(Home!)*
   Go back, from whence you came*(Home!)*
   My family tree, my family name*(Home!)*
   For some strange reason it had to be*(Home!)*
   He guided me to Tennessee.*(Home!)*
   Chorus

3. Now I see the importance of history
   Why my people be in the mess that they be
   Many journeys to freedom made in vain
   By brothers on the corner playin' ghetto games
   I ask you, Lord, why You enlightened me
   Without the enlightenment of all my folks
   He said, cuz I set myself on a quest for truth
   And He was there to quench my thirst
   But I am still thirsty
   The Lord allowed me to drink some more
   He said what I am searching for are
   The answers to all which are in front of me
   The ultimate truth started to get blurry
   For some strange reason it had to be
   It was all a dream about Tennessee.
   Chorus

THIS IS HOW WE DO IT

Words and Music by RICKY WALTERS,
OJI PIERCE and MONTELL JORDAN

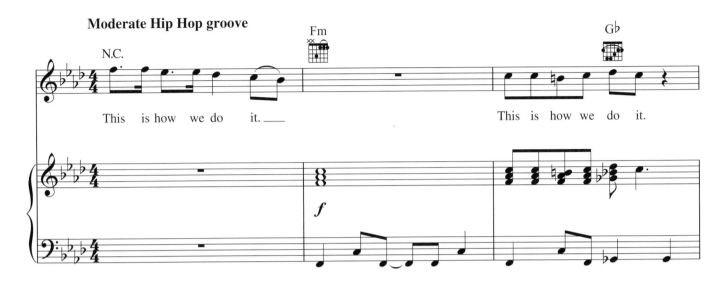

This is how we do it. ___ This is how we do it.

This is how we do it.

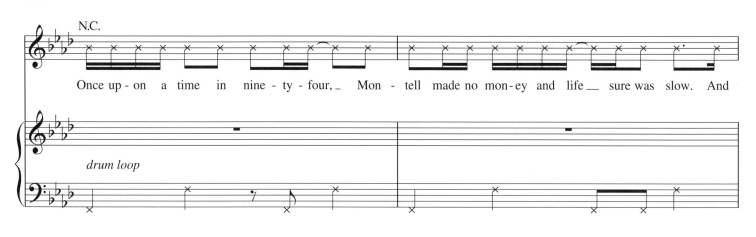

Once up-on a time in nine-ty-four, _ Mon-tell made no mon-ey and life _ sure was slow. And

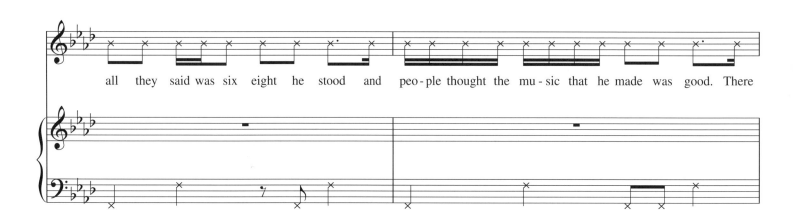

all they said was six eight he stood and peo-ple thought the mu-sic that he made was good. There

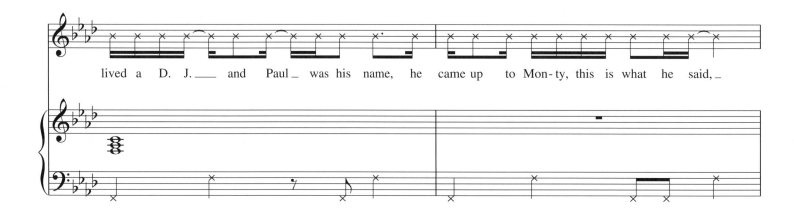

lived a D. J. _ and Paul _ was his name, he came up to Mon-ty, this is what he said, _

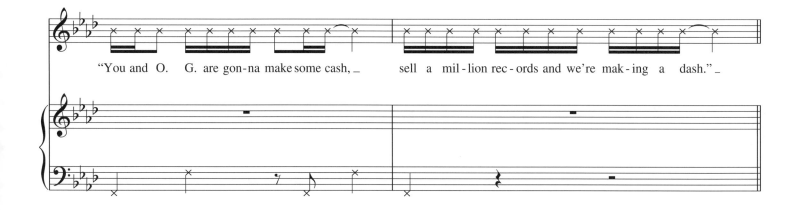

"You and O. G. are gon-na make some cash, _ sell a mil-lion rec-ords and we're mak-ing a dash." _

3 AM

Lyrics by ROB THOMAS
Music by ROB THOMAS, BRIAN YALE,
JOHN LESLIE GOFF and JOHN JOSEPH STANLEY

U CAN'T TOUCH THIS

Words and Music by RICK JAMES,
ALONZO MILLER and MC HAMMER

Fast Rap

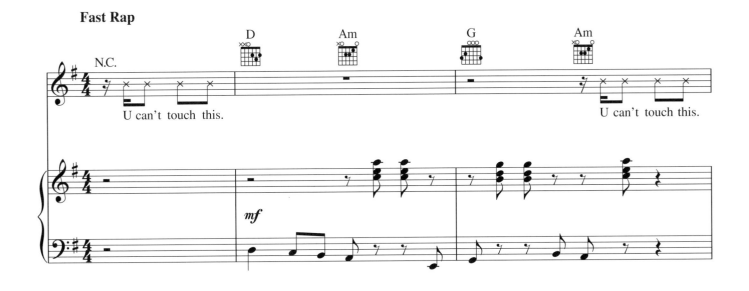

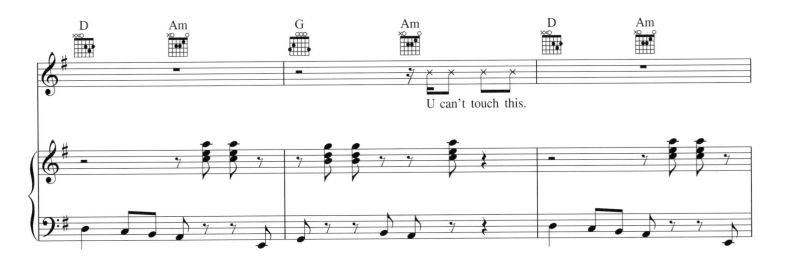

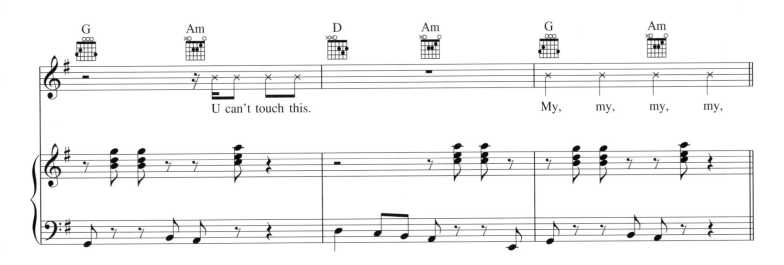

Rap Lyrics

Rap 1: My, my, my, my,
(Loop 1) Music hits me so hard.
Makes me say, "Oh, my Lord!"
Thank U for blessing me
With a mind to rhyme and two hyped feet.
It feels good when U know you're down
A super dope home boy from the "Oak"-town.
And I'm known as such,
And this is a beat, uh, U can't touch.

Chorus: I told U home boy,
(Loop 2) U can't touch this.
Yeah, that's how we're livin' and U know,
U can't touch this.
Look in my eyes, man,
U can't touch this.
Here, let me bust the funky lyrics,
U can't touch this.

Rap 2: Fresh new kicks and pants.
(Loop 1) U got it like that now U know U wanna dance.
So, move out of your seat and get a fly girl and
Catch this beat - while it's rollin'.
Hold on, pump a little bit
And let them know it's going on like that.
Like that cold on a mission, so fall on back.
Let 'em know that you're too much
And this is a beat U can't touch.

Chorus: Yo! I told U,
(Loop 2) U can't touch this.
Why U standin' there man?
U can't touch this.
Yo, sound the bells, school is in sucker,
U can't touch this.

Rap 3: Give me a song, or rhythm
(Loop 1) Making 'em sweat. That's what I'm giving 'em.
Now they know U talk about the Hammer,
You're talking about a show that' hyped.
And tight singers are sweating so pass them a wipe,
Or a tape to learn; what is it going to take
In the "90's" to burn the charts.
Legit. Either work hard or U might as well quit.
(To Chorus)

Rap 4: Go with the flow. It is said
(Loop 1) That if U can't groove to this, then U probably are dead.
So wave, your hands in the air.
Bust a few moves. Run your fingers through your hair.
This is it for a winner,
Dance to this an you're gonna get thinner.
Move. Slide your rump. Just for a minute, let's all do the bump.
Bump, bump.
(To Chorus)

Rap 5: Everytime U see me, the Hammer's just so hyped.
(Loop 1) I'm dope on the floor. And I'm magic on the mic.
Now why would I ever stop doing this?
When others making records that just don't hit.
I've toured around the world from London to the Bay.
It's Hammer, go Hammer, M.C. Hammer, yo Hammer,
And the rest can go and play.
(To Chorus)

GOOD RIDDANCE
(Time of Your Life)

Words by BILLIE JOE
Music by GREEN DAY

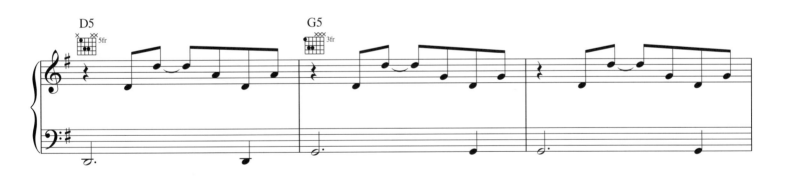

TWO PRINCES

Words and Music by
SPIN DOCTORS

UNDER THE BRIDGE

Words and Music by ANTHONY KIEDIS,
FLEA, JOHN FRUSCIANTE
and CHAD SMITH

487

is where I drew some blood. Under the bridge _ down-town

I could not get e - nough. _ Under the bridge _ down-town

for - got a - bout my love. Under the bridge _ down-town

I gave my life a - way. _____ *Vocal ad lib.*

Play 8 times

last time - rit.

UNBELIEVABLE

Words and Music by IAN DENCH,
JAMES ATKIN, ZACHARY FOLEY,
MARK DECLOEDT and DERRAN BROWNSON

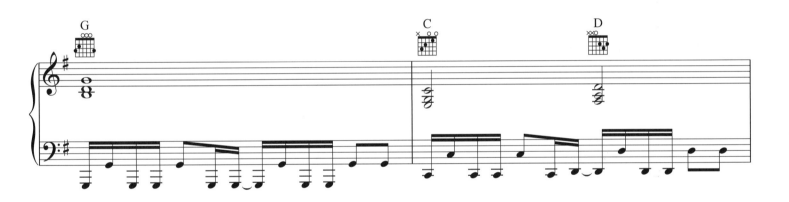

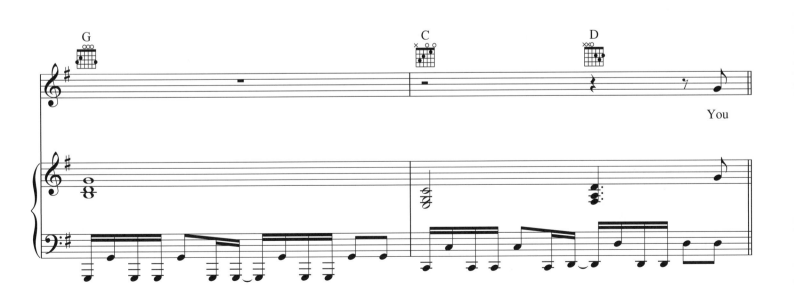

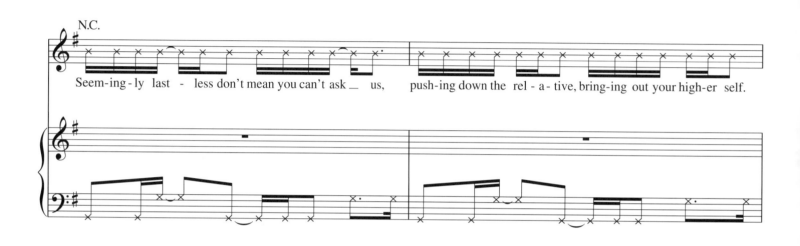

Seem-ing-ly last - less don't mean you can't ask __ us, push-ing down the rel - a - tive, bring-ing out your high-er self.

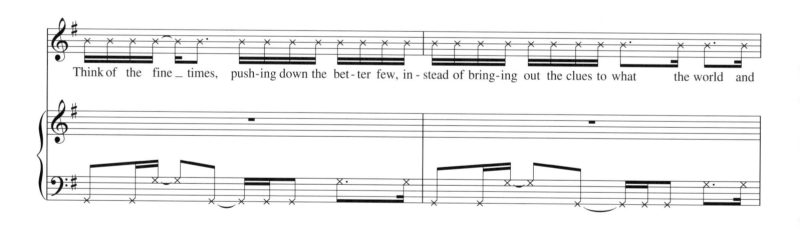

Think of the fine __ times, push-ing down the bet - ter few, in - stead of bring-ing out the clues to what the world and

ev - 'ry-thing your at - ti - tude, brace your-self __ with the grace of ease. __ I know __ this world __ ain't

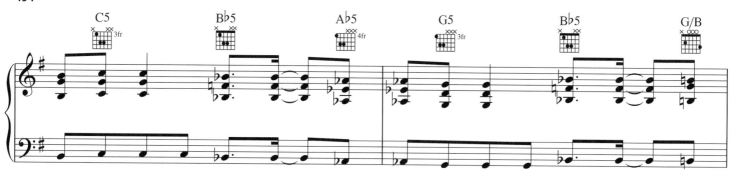

You're so un-be-liev - a-ble!

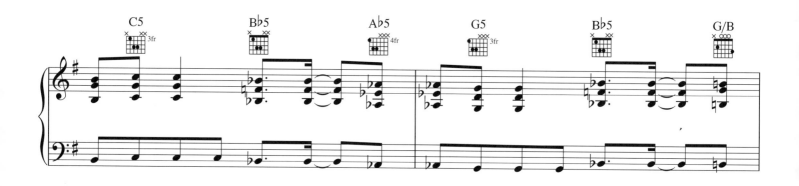

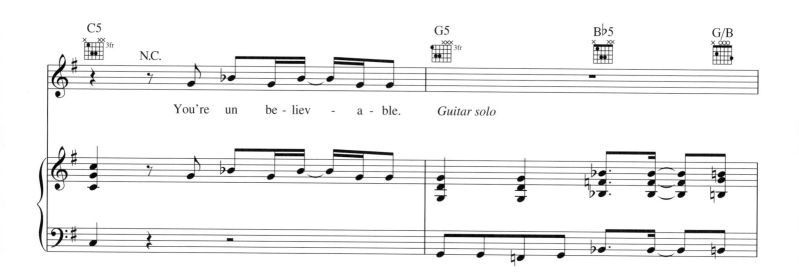

You're un be-liev - a-ble. *Guitar solo*

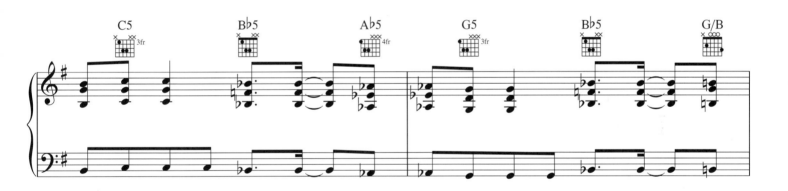

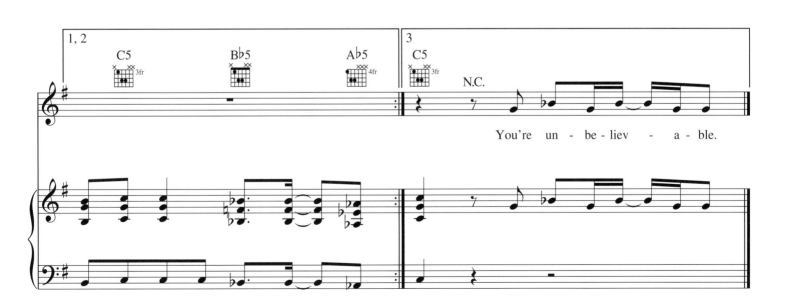

You're un - be - liev - a - ble.

VIRTUAL INSANITY

Words and Music by JASON KAY
and TOBY SMITH

* *Recorded a half step lower.*

WATERFALLS

Words and Music by MARQUEZE ETHERIDGE,
LISA NICOLE LOPES, RICO R. WADE,
PAT BROWN and RAMON MURRAY

E♭
B♭(add9)
D♭maj7
A♭(add9)/E♭
time he's in a jam she'll be by his side, but he does-n't re - al - ize he hurts her so much.
She gives him lov - ing that his bod - y can't han - dle, but all he can say is, "Ba - by, it's good
to me."
E♭maj7
B♭(add9)
But all the pray - ing just ain't help - ing at all, 'cause he can't
One day he goes and takes a glimpse in the mir - ror, but he
D♭maj7
A♭(add9)
E♭maj7
B♭(add9)
seem to keep his self out of trou - ble. So, he goes out and he makes his mon - ey the best
does - n't rec - og - nize his own face. His health is fad - ing and he
D♭maj7
A♭(add9)
way he knows how, an - oth - er bod - y lay - ing cold in the gut - ter. Lis - ten to me.
does - n't know why. Three let - ters took him to his fi - nal rest - ing place. Y'all don't hear me.

Additional Lyrics

Rap: I seen a rainbow yesterday
But too many storms have come and gone
Leavin' a trace of not one God-given ray
Is it because my life is ten shades of gray
I pray all ten fade away
Seldom praise Him for the sunny days
And like His promise is true
Only my faith can undo
The many chances I blew
To bring life to anew
Clear blue and unconditional skies
Have dried the tears from my eyes
No more lonely cries
My only bleedin' hope
Is for the folk who can't cope
Wit such an endurin' pain
That it keeps 'em in the pourin' rain
Who's to blame
For tootin' caine in your own vein
What a shame
You shoot and aim for someone else's brain
You claim the insane
And name this day in time
For fallin' prey to crime
I say the system got you victim to your own mind
Dreams are hopeless aspirations
In hopes of comin' true
Believe in yourself
The rest is up to me and you

VISION OF LOVE

Words and Music by MARIAH CAREY
and BEN MARGULIES

VOGUE

Words and Music by MADONNA CICCONE
and SHEP PETTIBONE

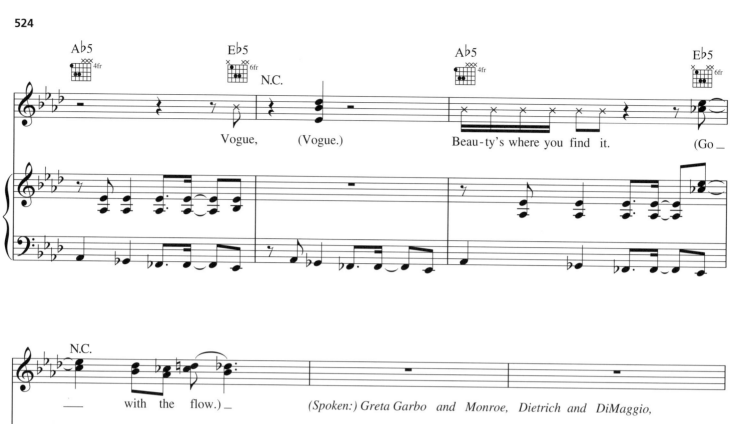

WANNABE

Words and Music by GERI HALLIWELL,
EMMA LEE BUNTON, MELANIE BROWN,
MELANIE CHISHOLM, VICTORIA BECKHAM,
MATT ROWEBOTTOM and RICHARD STANNARD

530

THE WAY

Words and Music by
TONY SCALZO

They made up their minds and they start-ed pack-ing. They left be-fore __ the sun __ came up __ that day, __ an

want-ed the high - way. They're hap-pi - er there to - day, ___ to - day. ___

To Coda

Their ___

An - y - one could see the

WHAT A MAN

Words and Music by
DAVID CRAWFORD

WONDERWALL

Words and Music by
NOEL GALLAGHER

WHO WILL SAVE YOUR SOUL

Lyrics and Music by
JEWEL KILCHER

Peo-ple liv-in' their lives for you __ on T - V. __ They say they're bet-ter than you, __ and you a - gree. __ He says "hold __ my calls" from be - hind those cold __ brick walls says, "Come here, boy, there ain't noth-in' for free." __

* *Originally sung an octave lower.*

D.S. al Coda

sav-ing our souls, __ a-fraid that God will take his toll that we for-get to be-gin. But,

CODA

N.C.

Some are walk - ing, some are talk -

- ing, some are stalk - ing their kill. Got So-cial Se-cu-ri-ty __ but it

YOU GET WHAT YOU GIVE

Words and Music by GREGG ALEXANDER
and RICK NOWELS

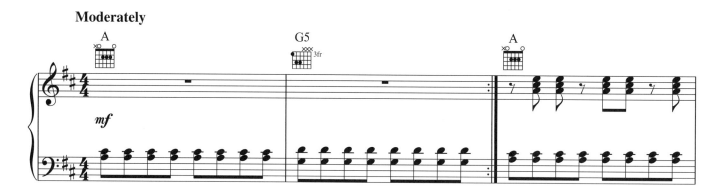

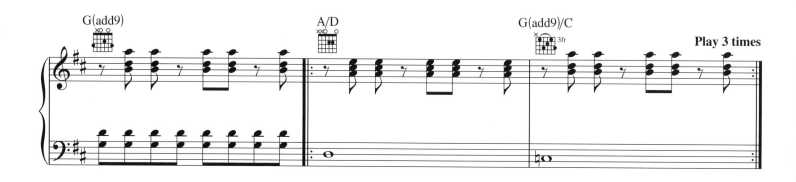

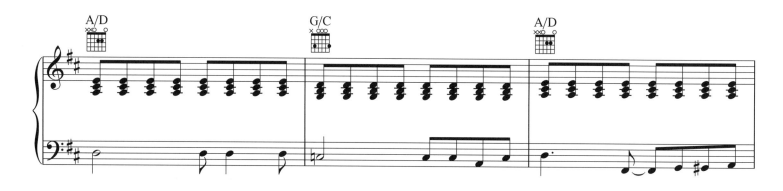

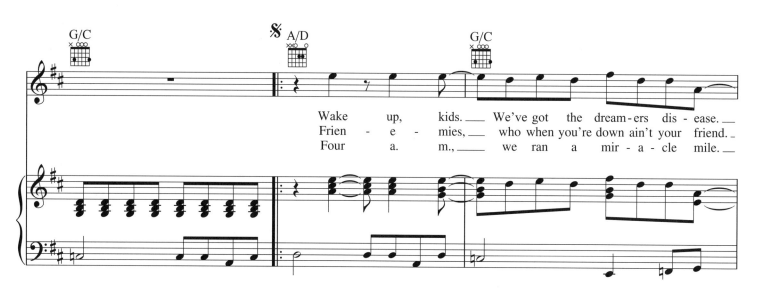

Wake up, kids. We've got the dream-ers dis - ease.
Frien - e - mies, who when you're down ain't your friend.
Four a. m., we ran a mir - a - cle mile.

YOU'RE STILL THE ONE

Words and Music by SHANIA TWAIN
and ROBERT JOHN LANGE

YOU OUGHTA KNOW

Lyrics by ALANIS MORISSETTE
Music by ALANIS MORISSETTE
and GLEN BALLARD

THE ULTIMATE SONGBOOKS

HAL•LEONARD

PIANO PLAY-ALONG

These great songbook/CD packs come with our standard arrangements for piano and voice with guitar chord frames plus a CD. The CD includes a full performance of each song, as well as a second track without the piano part so you can play "lead" with the band!

Vol. 1 Movie Music
00311072 P/V/G.....................$14.95

Vol. 2 Jazz Ballads
00311073 P/V/G.....................$14.95

Vol. 3 Timeless Pop
00311074 P/V/G.....................$14.95

Vol. 4 Broadway Classics
00311075 P/V/G $14.95

Vol. 5 Disney
00311076 P/V/G.....................$14.95

**Vol. 6
Country Standards**
00311077 P/V/G $14.95

Vol. 7 Love Songs
00311078 P/V/G.....................$14.95

Vol. 8 Classical Themes
00311079 Piano Solo $14.95

Vol. 9 Children's Songs
0311080 P/V/G $14.95

Vol. 10 Wedding Classics
00311081 Piano Solo.................$14.95

**Vol. 11
Wedding Favorites**
00311097 P/V/G $14.95

**Vol. 12
Christmas Favorites**
00311137 P/V/G.....................$14.95

**Vol. 13
Yuletide Favorites**
00311138 P/V/G.....................$14.95

Vol. 14 Pop Ballads
00311145 P/V/G.....................$14.95

**Vol. 15
Favorite Standards**
00311146 P/V/G.....................$14.95

Vol. 16 TV Classics
00311147 P/V/G.....................$14.95

Vol. 17 Movie Favorites
00311148 P/V/G.....................$14.95

Vol. 18 Jazz Standards
00311149 P/V/G.....................$14.95

**Vol. 19
Contemporary Hits**
00311162 P/V/G.....................$14.95

Vol. 20 R&B Ballads
00311163 P/V/G.....................$14.95

Vol. 21 Big Band
00311164 P/V/G.....................$14.95

Vol. 22 Rock Classics
00311165 P/V/G.....................$14.95

Vol. 23 Worship Classics
00311166 P/V/G.....................$14.95

Vol. 24 Les Misérables
00311169 P/V/G.....................$14.95

**Vol. 25
The Sound of Music**
00311175 P/V/G.....................$14.95

**Vol. 26 Andrew Lloyd
Webber Favorites**
00311178 P/V/G.....................$14.95

**Vol. 27 Andrew Lloyd
Webber Greats**
00311179 P/V/G.....................$14.95

**Vol. 28
Lennon & McCartney**
00311180 P/V/G.....................$14.95

Vol. 29 The Beach Boys
00311181 P/V/G.....................$14.95

Vol. 30 Elton John
00311182 P/V/G.....................$14.95

Vol. 31 Carpenters
00311183 P/V/G.....................$14.95

**Vol. 32
Bacharach & David**
00311218 P/V/G.....................$14.95

Vol. 33 Peanuts™
00311227 P/V/G.....................$14.95

**Vol. 34 Charlie Brown
Christmas**
00311228 P/V/G.....................$14.95

**Vol. 35
Elvis Presley Hits**
00311230 P/V/G.....................$14.95

**Vol. 36
Elvis Presley Greats**
00311231 P/V/G.....................$14.95

**Vol. 37 Contemporary
Christian**
00311232 P/V/G.....................$14.95

**Vol. 38 Duke Ellington –
Standards**
00311233 P/V/G.....................$14.95

**Vol. 39 Duke Ellington –
Classics**
00311234 P/V/G.....................$14.95

Vol. 40 Showtunes
00311237 P/V/G.....................$14.95

**Vol. 41
Rodgers & Hammerstein**
00311238 P/V/G.....................$14.95

Vol. 42 Irving Berlin
00311339 P/V/G.....................$14.95

Vol. 43 Jerome Kern
00311340 P/V/G.....................$14.95

**Vol. 44 Frank Sinatra –
Popular Hits**
00311377 P/V/G.....................$14.95

**Vol. 45 Frank Sinatra –
Most Requested Songs**
00311378 P/V/G.....................$14.95

Vol. 46 Wicked
00311317 P/V/G.....................$14.95

Vol. 47 Rent
00311319 P/V/G.....................$14.95

**Vol. 48
Christmas Carols**
00311332 P/V/G.....................$14.95

Vol. 49 Holiday Hits
00311333 P/V/G.....................$14.95

**Vol. 51
High School Musical**
00311421 P/V/G.....................$19.95

**Vol. 52 Andrew Lloyd
Webber Classics**
00311422 P/V/G.....................$14.95

Vol. 53 Grease
00311450 P/V/G.....................$14.95

**Vol. 54
Broadway Favorites**
00311451 P/V/G.....................$14.95

Vol. 55 The 1940s
00311453 P/V/G.....................$14.95

Vol. 56 The 1950s
00311459 P/V/G.....................$14.95

**Vol. 63
High School Musical 2**
00311470 P/V/G.....................$19.95

**Vol. 64
God Bless America**
00311489 P/V/G.....................$14.95

Vol. 65 Casting Crowns
00311494 P/V/G.....................$14.95

FOR MORE INFORMATION, SEE YOUR LOCAL MUSIC DEALER,
OR WRITE TO:

7777 W. BLUEMOUND RD. P.O. BOX 13819 MILWAUKEE, WI 53213
Visit Hal Leonard Online at **www.halleonard.com**

Prices, contents, and availability subject to change without notice.
Disney characters and artwork © Disney Enterprises, Inc.

0108